BIG IDEAS

Big Ideas

The Essential Guide to
the Latest Thinking

JAMES HARKIN

Atlantic Books

First published as a Paperback Original in Great Britain in 2008 by

Atlantic Books,
an imprint of Grove Atlantic, Inc.

9 8 7 6 5 4 3 2 1

A CIP catalogue record for this book is available from the British
Library.

ISBN 978 1 84354 710 5

Printed in Great Britain
Atlantic Books
An imprint of Grove Atlantic Ltd.
Ormond House
26–27 Boswell Street
London WC1N 3JZ

Contents

Introduction

What can it mean to be a 'libertarian paternalist', a 'slacktivist' or a 'transhumanist'? How does 'peer-to-peer' surveillance differ from ordinary snooping, and where can one go about finding a 'virtual anthropologist'? What is it like to live in an 'experience economy'? When people murmur knowingly about something called 'the wisdom of crowds', what are they talking about? Is there really a 'tipping point' in every field of human endeavour, and, if so, where does it come from and how does it work?

Assaulted by a battery of new ideas, buzzwords and neologisms, it is easy to feel left out. In the last few years, after several decades during which grand, overarching political ideologies were overthrown and ideas of any stripe were treated with suspicion, an esoteric new vocabulary of ideas bobbed back to the surface of social life and began to appear on everyone's lips. These new kinds of ideas came in different shapes and sizes. There were ideas as labels to help us describe and understand our changing world and the people in it; ideas as innovations to help us to change things; ideas to help turn businesses around and make money; most of all, there were ideas to make us, our organizations and our politicians more novel and more exciting. All of a sudden, it seemed, ideas – big, weighty, serious-sounding ideas – were the most fashionable currency in town, and everyone seemed to want one of their own.

One catalyst for this, in the world of politics at least, was a broad shifting of the tectonic plates and the sense of an era coming to an end. In North America and Europe, incumbent governments – George Bush's administration in North America, Tony Blair's New Labour project in Britain, Jacques Chirac's Presidency of France – began to look flailing and unwieldy, as if they were about to give way to something else. If the new generation of political contenders – not only David Cameron in the UK, but Nicolas Sarkozy in France and Barack Obama in the United States – did nothing else, they added a little intellectual Viagra back into political debate. They also did something to resuscitate the principle that ideas – abstractions which hover over and shape debates about what governments do – matter after all. Without ideas, everything is random: politicians are mere opportunists, coming up with arbitrary policy wheezes that bear no relationship to one another; policy prescriptions are nothing but focus groups writ large; delivery, polish and execution are everything. Thankfully, we have lost our patience with all that. The pressing questions at the beginning of the twenty-first century – among them the way that we approach risk and uncertainty, the state of the environment, the make-up of national identity, the nature and meaning of political terrorism, the progress of globalization and the politics of human rights – are very different from those in the past, but just as prone to riddle and wrong-headedness. They demand new ideas, bold concepts and fresh thinking.

But where would that thinking come from? Not from academic philosophers, for sure. Anglo-Saxon philosophers, steeped in the 'ordinary language' school of analytical philosophy, have long been suspicious of ideas of any stripe, which they saw as no more than an unwarranted fit of continental European enthusiasm.

Their job, as they saw it, was to take ideas which already happened to exist – justice, liberty, etc. – and then refine and sharpen them into something which made sense. For these kinds of philosophers, big ideas were only raw materials, waiting to be burnished and buffed up by themselves into something approaching internal coherence. They were not much interested in thinking up ideas themselves. Ask them for one, and they were likely to reply that it was not their job.

Much better placed to think up big ideas were the continental European philosophers, whose initial enchantment with ideas about society and culture was as intense as their irritation with the pedantry of Anglo-Saxon philosophy. It was they, after all, who revelled in the grand ideas of Hegel, Marx and Freud and made them their own. No sooner had they inculcated us in their sweeping intellectual narratives, however, than they promptly spat them out. In 1984, for example, the French philosopher and former Marxist Jean-François Lyotard argued that grand ideologies or 'metanarratives' – if those were intended to order and explain all our knowledge and experience – had outlived their usefulness. What we were left with was 'postmodernism' – Lyotard defined this as 'an incredulity towards metanarratives' – which was sceptical of anything which purported to explain too much. Like many other left-leaning intellectuals during the last two decades, Lyotard spent much of his time feasting on the rotting carcass of twentieth-century ideologies like Marxism and socialism. These 'Post-it' intellectuals were largely successful in their mission to kick ideologies when they were on the way down, but their mission was almost wholly destructive. Very soon, however, we tired of verbose, dissembling intellectuals who wanted to tell us only what could not be understood. Anyone who talks too loosely about 'postmodernism' or 'post-structuralism' is nowadays themselves treated with a healthy dose of scepticism.

THE NEW LANDSCAPE OF IDEAS

Anyone looking to politicians or to university-based ideologues to stimulate new thinking, however, was looking in the wrong place. Long before Cameron, Obama and Sarkozy had become regular fixtures on our television sets, the media had detected an appetite for big ideas and, for those who cared to look, there was plenty of interest in new ideas around. The success of idea books like *The Tipping Point* and *Freakonomics* and a huge glut of books about happiness all signified to cultural commissars a thirst for good ideas clearly expressed. It became fashionable to establish an 'ideas factory' or 'ideas laboratory' within organizations, as if it were somehow possible to punch out ideas on an industrial scale. This thirst for new ideas spread to newspapers and magazines. The *New Yorker*, buoyed up by staff writers like Malcolm Gladwell, James Surowiecki and Louis Menand, developed an enviable reputation for helping to explain complex ideas to a lay audience. In the year 2000, the *New York Times* even inaugurated an annual 'ideas of the year' supplement, handing out gongs to the best new ideas around the world. In the UK, newspapers like the *Guardian*, the *Financial Times* and magazines like the *New Statesman* joined in, investing in 'ideas' columns whose job it was to navigate the deluge of new ideas which were being thrown their way.

This global market for new ideas began to move at breakneck speed. Good ideas had always been contagious, but thanks to the internet and the increasingly globalized media, new ideas and buzzwords – borrowed or shamelessly ripped off – were making their way around the world almost as soon as they were invented. As the new global landscape of ideas began to settle, something else became clear too. In the new marketplace for ideas, North America was way out in front. If distinctively European thinkers like Isaiah Berlin and emigrés from Europe to America like Hannah Arendt had dominated the battleground of ideas during the age of ideology (defined by the British historian Eric Hobsbawm as the years between the First World War and the fall of the Berlin Wall), one of the oddities of this new landscape of ideas was that the Americans seemed to be better at generating them. There were still some heavyweight moral and political philosophers around in Europe with novel things to say – Jürgen Habermas in Germany, Slavoj Žižek in Slovenia, Jean Baudrillard in France, for example – but they were few and far. When Baudrillard died in March 2007, at the age of seventy-seven, it seemed to signify the close of an intellectual era. Baudrillard, hero to the polo-necked, pointy-spectacled classes, had made it his life's work to argue that, under the weight of our relentless consumption of objects and media, simulated experiences had come to replace the real thing and reality and fantasy had blurred into one impenetrable edifice called 'hyper-reality'. He was much scoffed at by Anglophone philosophers for his efforts, but at least he took the trouble to engage with the real world, even if he didn't believe it was entirely real. In any case, Baudrillard was canny enough to know which way the intellectual wind blew. For all his criticism of American culture, he was enchanted by this place he called 'the original version of modernity'. France, he pointed out, was nothing more than 'a copy with subtitles'.

So why did the centre of gravitas shift towards America? One reason was the deep pockets of America's think tanks and its universities, the resources and reputations of which were able to attract the world's best thinkers and afford them the time to cogitate and write at their leisure. For example, in 2003 the controversial American libertarian think-tanker and fellow of the American Enterprise Institute Charles Murray published a book called *Human Accomplishment; The Pursuit of Excellence in the Arts and Sciences, 800 BC to 1950*, a huge tome full of graphs and tables in which Murray tried to rank the top 4,000 thinkers in human history. Setting aside the eccentricities of Murray's project for a moment, can anyone imagine a think tank in Europe with the resources and the confidence to allow one of its scholars to spend five years on a project as unashamedly intellectual as this?

But if America's dominance in the new global landscape of ideas was partly due to the pulling power of its universities and think tanks, it was also because Americans had become expert packagers of ideas. More than anywhere else in the world, American writers and thinkers seemed to have the knack of explaining complex ideas in an accessible way for a popular audience. Perhaps it was the fact that journalism in America was taken more seriously than it was in most other countries. Or maybe it was all in the branding, the discovery of that headline title or gimmick – 'Freakonomics', 'The Tipping Point', 'The Wisdom of Crowds' – which captured the essence of a complicated idea while intriguing the reader enough to read more. To cite an example: for a brief period in autumn 2006, the global media became very excited about the merits of a new book called *The J Curve*. Penned by an American political scientist called Ian Bremmer, the book purported to offer an account of how nations that emerge from authoritarianism go through a period of instability and disorder before they settle into a stable democracy. It was a rather pedestrian idea, and doubtless would have sunk without trace had it not been for two things. It helped, of course, that the book was published at a time when ruling elites in Britain and America were beginning to entertain serious doubts about their invasion of Iraq. But that wasn't the only reason Bremmer's book did well. Its title – *The J Curve* – seemed to suggest something impressively scientific and yet unutterably obvious about how countries take their first steps from dictatorship to democracy. If it had been written by a European academic, it would undoubtedly have been called 'Dictatorships in Transition: Towards a theory of the transition to post-authoritarian democracies', and would, as a result, have withered in the political science section of some of our more comprehensive bookshops. As it was, it cleaned up.

There was something else going on in the world of ideas, too. While academic output became ever more specialized, a new kind of professional emerged to take up the burden of talking about big ideas and thinking through social trends. Almost overnight, it seemed, we were confronted by legions of ideas salesmen – ideas entrepreneurs, media gurus, think-tankers and policy wonks, features journalists and talking heads, demographers and marketers, technologists, management theorists, futurologists and trend forecasters – whose job it became to think up easily digestible abstractions that might help to explain society and the terms of public debate. The think-tankers borrowed from Harvard professors like Robert Putnam and Mark Moore apparently hard-headed ideas like 'social capital' and 'public value' to make their work sound more respectable. The future-gazers rhapsodized about the accelerating pace of social change. The technologists forgot about society completely and instead talked up the idea that the new technologies would make distance disappear and allow products of all kinds to be customized to our individual taste. The demographers and marketers, meanwhile, set about slicing and dicing the populations into smaller and smaller categories with ever-increasing enthusiasm.

Much of it was tendentious rubbish, the tossed-off generalizations of intellectual chancers. But it would be a mistake to dismiss entirely this new breed of ideas professional. Unlike some academics, the new idea-makers lacked verbosity or obscurantism. They were well practised at expressing their ideas clearly, and most of their ideas were simple enough to be expressed in a couple of paragraphs – which is why their books, when they got around to writing them, tended to be puffed up with more padding than a lingerie model's bra. Their ideas might announce themselves in a gimmicky way, but those same ideas and the empirical research behind them could teach us a good deal about changes in the public mood and intellectual fashions. Trace the connections between them and they added up to something approximating a distinctively twenty-first century ideology. When the *New York Times* journalist Thomas Friedman shoehorned a variety of different trends into an awkward but informative thesis that 'The World is Flat', he was talking about the same revolt against hierarchies that motivated technologists to enthuse about the growing import of 'peer-to-peer' communications. When marketers talked up something called 'buzz marketing', they were championing exactly the same word-of-mouth phenomenon that Malcolm Gladwell, in his book *The Tipping Point*, had likened to a contagious virus. When researchers stopped celebrating how wonderful it was to be a 'singleton' and started referring to the same people as 'regretful loners', it told us a good deal about shifts in social attitudes to single living.

Any attempt to understand the contemporary world, then, needs to be broad-minded enough to sift through ideas of all kinds. But it is equally important to go armed with a razor-sharp bullshit detector. Government, the professions and the corporate world are now knee-deep in faddish ideas that appear with a fanfare before being mercilessly discarded like old toys. No sooner has one been purged than another has arisen to take its place. It helps that faddish concepts – usually based around mini-ideas like 'empowerment', 'positive thinking', or 'emotional intelligence' – are the lifeblood of a burgeoning cadre of management consultants, the witch doctors of the modern workplace.

BIG IDEAS: A HOW-TO GUIDE

How, then, can we measure the worth of an idea? Is it its intrinsic rightness or validity, or its power and the elegance with which it is expressed? One important measure of the worth of an idea about society is how far it ricochets through the culture and makes its presence felt. Ideas are in the ether; very often they are arrived at in different ways and in different places, in different disciplines and in different hierarchies of knowledge at around the same time. When the biologist Richard Dawkins developed his idea about a 'selfish gene' thirty years ago, he imported into genetics a highly contestable theory about human behaviour called game theory – and its most famous game, the prisoner's dilemma – which was being touted around by American economists, and which had been in turn borrowed from mathematicians. When, more recently, the former American Defense

Secretary Donald Rumsfeld made his infamous speech about the 'known unknowns' when dealing with Iraq's hypothetical weapons of mass destruction, he was articulating exactly the same spectral aversion to uncertainty that European sociologists have filed under the heading 'risk society' and that European think-tankers know as 'the precautionary principle'.

If interesting ideas are all around us, the real trick is how to find an audience for them. Even if it is expertly packaged, however, an idea needs to have some substance if it is to have a chance of succeeding in the intellectual marketplace. What kind of ideas are doing well? The new ideas men and women were much less interested in grand schematic thinking about how societies worked than their predecessors. Rather, what fascinated them were the foibles and idiosyncrasies of human behaviour and how – with a little prior knowledge and a few handy hints – it might be possible to nudge that behaviour in a more fortuitous direction. They also tended to shamelessly mix up disciplines in an apparently iconoclastic way.

For some years now, the hottest research area within economics has been behavioural economics – a hybrid of economics with social psychology which sets out to understand real human behaviour within markets and demolish the clean-cut assumptions about human rationality made by conventional neo-classical economists. Very often it pays to bring science into the mix – in recent years, the public has been subjected to a fusion of science and art called 'sci-art', an attempted meshing of neuroscience and economics called 'neuroeconomics' and a controversial new hybrid of science and theology called 'neurotheology'. Then there is the network theory invented by Manuel Castells, which has now expanded its empire from science and computing into just about every field of human understanding. This laudable urge to join the dots between disciplines often stems from a rather sorry disillusionment among thinkers with the potential of their own discipline – and particularly the social sciences – to understand the world. Sometimes these attempts at imaginative fusion are simply nonsense on stilts, but they manage to turn intellectual heads all the same.

In the place of grand projects to change society, it would be fair to say, ideas had retreated to the more modest study of human behaviour at the micro-scale and how to change it. What remains impressive about the new crop of ideas, however, is the direction in which they are running. If the prevailing ideology since the era of Margaret Thatcher has been that there is no such thing as society, the real intellectual action in this decade has been to go beyond the fundamental axiom of neo-classical economics, the idea that each of us is an isolated individual concerned only to maximize our own advantage and understand afresh the dynamics of social or collective behaviour. The fundamental idea at the heart of Malcolm Gladwell's *The Tipping Point*, for example, is one which tries to explain how ideas and rumours are passed from one person to another.

In their books *The Wisdom of Crowds* and *Critical Mass* the journalist James Surowiecki and the science writer Philip Ball had a crack at explaining the sometimes unpredictable behaviour of crowds, and in the burgeoning discipline of network theory thinkers try to comprehend communities by imagining them as vast networks of connections. All of this represents a renewed interest in society, albeit at the expense of throwing out most of the intellectual armoury amassed by the social sciences in favour of techniques and analogies drawn from technology or the natural sciences. For Malcolm Gladwell humans are viruses which are prone to starting epidemics; for Philip Ball we are all gas particles prone to condensing abruptly into water; for the network theorists we are all lonely nodes hoping to bump into one another on a network. This renewed focus on what binds us together is entirely welcome; society, after all, has to be more than the sum of its parts. But the horizons of many of these ideas are nevertheless limited. What they suggest is that society is complex and potentially combustible, that interventions in it are prone to give rise to unintended consequences – and that change can be achieved only tentatively and at the margins, by gently nudging us blind, formless masses in one direction or another.

It can hardly be a coincidence that this is also the message that we hear on the lips of our politicians. Many of them, after all, have cherry-picked their ideas from think tanks, ideas entrepreneurs, demographers and marketing consultants. Ambitious politicians on both sides of the Atlantic, even those whose intellectual heritage is steeped in a rugged, narrowly economic libertarianism, are keen to rehabilitate the idea of society and point out that it does exist after all – but that it is battered, traumatized, ill at ease with itself and, a bit like Humpty Dumpty, in need of being put back together again. The new political ideas, as a consequence, are all about finding ways to make this happen. They make liberal use of buzzwords like 'social responsibility', 'active citizenship', 'sustainability' and 'community'. The proposals they usher forth include everything from making more use of the voluntary and charitable sectors, to rejigging the tax-and-benefit incentives on offer to encourage people to behave in more responsible ways. All this is well and good, but it smacks of a narrow managerialism whose approach to motivating its citizenry is a simple matter of neat technical fixes like economic carrots and sticks. It is not enough for politicians to tell us that society is bruised and in need of some attention. The only things capable of really reinvigorating political society are ideas which could bring people together with a shared purpose. New ideas like liberty, equality and fraternity were the motivating principles of the French Revolution, and a brand new idea about how social welfare and a healthy economy could go hand in hand was the impetus behind the birth of the welfare state. Both managed to inspire people in their time. We could do with being inspired again.

All this might sound idealistic, but maybe a little idealism is not such a bad thing. When the leading philosopher of German idealism, Georg Wilhelm Friedrich Hegel, was thinking and writing in the early nineteenth century, he wasn't floating woolly utopian schemes for the perfectability of human nature. What he meant by idealism was that our ideas about things are just as, if not more important than the things themselves, because they create those things and help determine the world that we live in. Ideas are like a boomerang – give up on them or hurl them disdainfully into the middle distance and they are likely to come back and hit you in the back of the head. Those who think they can sneer at them or shrug them off, after all, are usually the same people who routinely wave rather bad ideas through on the nod.

Any survey of contemporary ideas is bound to reflect the biases and prejudices of the author. This one, however, is designed to be broad enough to give a coherent snapshot of the world in which we live and its ideas of itself. Given that it is impossible to rid ourselves of the ideas which motivate us to action, it surely behoves us to scrutinize them more closely and to think up better ones – not just ideas to live by, or to make a quick buck out of, but to grasp the world with and change it for the better. Think big, think bold – because the ideas that you have are more powerful and more influential than you think.

The Advocacy Revolution

Ever heard of the Association of British Drivers? According to its website, the ABD is a voluntary and non-profit group funded by subscriptions – it charges an annual fee of twenty pounds – from ordinary drivers. It is a little coy about how many members it has, but when the *Guardian* newspaper launched an investigation into its affairs in 2004, it claimed that it had 2,256 paid-up members. That is not very many. There are nearly 32 million drivers in Britain, after all, so even according to its own statistics, the ABD numbers among its membership only 0.007 per cent of those in its membership. How can a body which purports to represent the interests of British drivers have so few of those drivers on its books?

In the last twenty years, the number of pressure and lobby groups have mushroomed in most Western countries. The most obvious growth has been amongst those who, like the ABD, claim to influence the political process on behalf of the interests of a particular social group. The problem is that many of them are not what they claim to be. Take another ludicrous example, this time from the United States. The American Association of Single People (AASP) is an organization which claims to represent the interests of America's 86 million single people, making sure they don't get ripped off when booking hotels, or ignored when governments come to set taxes. What it doesn't shout about is that only one out of every 54,666 of American singletons has bothered to join.

What can be done? Some clues can be found in the work of the Harvard sociologist Theda Skocpol. In her book *Diminished Democracy: From Membership to Management in American Civic Life* (2003), Skocpol draws our attention to an arresting but scarcely remarked-upon paradox in contemporary political life: that there are more organizing groups around than ever before but with fewer real participants. Political influence, she claims, has ebbed away from communities and voluntary associations towards professionally managed advocacy groups.

In a forensic analysis of American political history, Skocpol notes that membership of organizations such as trade unions and churches dominated civic life in the US from the late nineteenth century until the middle of the twentieth. Such groups oiled the wheels of democracy in more ways than one, she argues: they opened up spaces where ordinary people could debate the issues and trained their members in democratic procedures like conducting elections and serving in office. All that changed in the 1960s, however, when those groups began to be replaced by 'memberless entities' or 'mailing list organizations' that saw little need for democratic participation and in which membership meant no more than signing a cheque or ticking a box. Democracy was kidnapped by professional managers and lobbyists, and diminished as a result.

What made it happen? Skocpol points to the proliferation of watchdogs and regulatory agencies and the growing role of law in politics during the 1960s and 1970s, which made mass involvement cumbersome and unnecessary. Who needs members, after all, when you can hire underlings to draft legislation, lobbyists to befriend parliamentarians and PRs to spin your cause to the media? 'America,' argues Skocpol, 'is now full of civic entrepreneurs who are constantly looking upward for potential angels, schmoozing with the wealthy.'

But it is not all bad news. Some argue the grassroots politics that were trampled by insiderism and professionalism can be refurbished with new social movements based on the web – so-called 'net roots'. Liberal activist group MoveOn.org in America, with nearly three million members, is often floated as an example. Clicking with a mouse, however, is scarcely more credible a form of democratic deliberation than posting a cheque. Worse, both mailing list organizations and net-based movements tend to favour the cash-rich, time-poor, who are more likely to enjoy this kind of participation by proxy.

Skocpol's intriguing suggestion is that if more organizations asked ordinary citizens to actually do something, they might be pleasantly surprised. Meanwhile, it would help if memberless organizations like the Association of British Drivers and the American Association of Singe People came clean – and admitted that they are representative of no one but themselves.

Badvertising

The problem with watching television advertisements nowadays is that you never know how it is all going to end. A beautiful and smartly dressed young woman showing you around her palatial home might be selling furniture or mobile phones, but something about her makes you a little wary. Maybe it is because she looks a little clueless, a little disposable. Sure enough, she has scarcely stepped out to the shops when a passing car butts her high into the air. She lands in the street, stone dead and with blood trickling from her nose.

Welcome to the unsettling new world of badvertising. Time was when advertising promised to raise our aspirations – to lull us into a lifestyle daydream hitched to whatever the advertisers needed to flog. Just recently, however, we can add to that something quite different – a mini-industry of government health and safety films, whose job it is not to sell us a consumerist fantasy but to warn us of the disastrous consequences of our actions. The politics and aesthetics come from an unusual source. Badvertising has its origins in the American and Canadian anti-corporate movement of the 1990s, when radical advertisers and designers tried to alleviate their consciences by working to flip the message of mainstream ads. Highlights of their subversive artwork were published in magazines such as *Adbusters* or by websites such as the BADvertising Institute. They included a vodka bottle embossed with the slogan 'Absolut Nonsense', and a spoof on a Tommy Hilfiger campaign featuring a herd of sheep and the tag line 'Tommy follow the Herd'. Where the anti-advertisers really excelled was in subverting traditional ad campaigns by pointing out the harmful effects of products: having Marlboro Man wheezing into an asthma inhaler, for example, or putting him and his legendary horse into twin beds in the cancer ward.

Since the rise of sophisticated public health campaigns aimed at changing our behaviour over the past couple of years, the baton of badvertising has passed firmly to government, which has been quite happy to learn both strategy and methods from the anti-advertisers. Just as the advertisers of cigarettes were teased by the anti-advertising activists with the threat of impotence, now public health campaigns routinely assure us that smoking is neither big or clever – and that if we don't give it up, very soon we won't be able to get it up.

The problem with badvertising is that it can be just as deceitful and manipulative as any other kind of advertising. When badvertisers tell us that smoking will make us impotent, or that driving home after a drink may cause us to mow down a zebra crossing full of schoolchildren, they are not giving us the statistical facts but selling us a line. Badvertising, it turns out, is hampered by the same ethical problems as traditional advertising – and is far more unpleasant to watch.

Bare Branches

Counting up the numbers of boys and girls in a country has never been so troublesome. At the beginning of 2006, the medical journal the *Lancet* published a report estimating that prenatal selection and selective abortion in India was likely to be causing half a million girls to be culled every year. Within twenty-four hours, the Indian medical association weighed in to dispute the *Lancet*'s figures as out of date and exaggerated. The Indian government made no formal statement, but was said to be incandescent with rage.

There were good reasons for all this sensitivity. The abnormally unbalanced gender ratios of some Asian countries – either due to abortion, sex-selective technologies such as ultrasound or old-fashioned infanticide – have been the subject of academic controversy since the late 1980s. Just recently, however, they have come to be cloaked in a more sinister hue. One of the new growth areas in academia is in 'security demographics', where scholars are invited to predict the potentially dire implications of demographic change, and one of the most gloomy prognostications is rooted in what could happen when sex ratios spin out of kilter. 'Bare branches' is the Chinese term for the poor young men who are left with no prospect of finding a partner or starting a family. In their influential 2004 book of the same name, the American political scientists Valerie M. Hudson and Andrea M. den Boer argued that these surplus men are a social catastrophe in the making. The pair found evidence of a huge number of 'missing females' in Bangladesh, China, India, Nepal, Pakistan, Taiwan, South Korea and Vietnam. Most of the authors' attention, however, is reserved for China and India, where two-fifths of the world's population now live and where active or passive infanticide is prevalent.

These legions of surplus males, according to Hudson and den Boer, are often poor or unemployed, and lack bargaining power in the market for marriage. The consequences of this vast demographic shift could be dire. As economies turn bad, those surplus males are likely to generate crime and violence. One way for countries to absorb the growing surfeit of young males, they argue, might be to amass huge armies and go to war. 'In 2020,' Hudson predicts, 'it may seem to China that it would be worth it to have a very bloody battle in which a lot of their young men could die in some glorious cause.' Nor will all this do much to improve the lot of women. Since females in such societies lack bargaining power, their relative scarcity means only that they are more likely to be kidnapped or sold to order.

Hudson and den Boer's thesis makes intriguing reading, but it is nothing more than an imaginative worst-case scenario. India has sought to stem the tide of sex selection by banning the use of technology to determine the sex of foetuses, but technology can usually outwit regulation. And although doctors in India must not tell the couples the sex of their foetus, many have developed coded signals for the job instead. The real reasons for the imbalance in the gender of babies lie in the hand-to-mouth agrarian culture of many parts of India, where men's physical labour counts for more than that of women and marriage dowries are excruciatingly expensive. The answer to 'bare branches' lies not in bans, but in rapid development into the kind of world that has more time for the delicate charms of little girls.

Boomergeddon

The latest tour by the Rolling Stones was the most popular in history. Between August 2005 and November 2006, the band played 110 shows in front of 3.5 million fans, and made themselves a cool £226 millions. That the Stones are still allowed on stage at all is a shining example of what the music journalist John Strausbaugh has dubbed 'colostomy rock' – the continued weight exerted by baby-boomers on what was previously thought of as youth culture.

The term 'baby-boomers' is essentially an American invention,

7

used to describe the unusually large cohort of babies born between 1946 and 1964 in a surge of post-war optimism. Both British and American boomers are now hurtling through the demographic turnstile towards retirement, and the first of them hit sixty in 2006. Since they have revolutionized every stage of life through which they have passed, say the pundits, they are set to 'update' the business of growing old.

Now, inevitably, comes a thundering backlash. 'Balding, Wrinkled and Stoned' was the less-than-flattering strapline for a *Time* magazine article in February 2006, one which painted a picture of a generation whose continued proclivity for illicit drugs is embarrassing even their children. In a barrage of books, too, social critics from both right and left are taking aim at the new middle-aged. 'Boomergeddon' is the not-too-subtle working title of a new book being written by the American sociologist Mike Males. In it, Males agrees that American boomers have smuggled their free-thinking, hell-raising values into middle age, but argues that, as a result, they are the fastest growing demographic group to be involved in serious crime and the most likely to have HIV.

In his book *Balsamic Dreams*, the American satirist and baby-boomer Joe Queenan also has a pop at his own generation, accusing them of self-importance, narcissism and selling out. The boomers, he argues, lived it up on state subsidies in their salad days and are now determined to kick away the ladder of social security for everyone else. Their determination to be different, he says, has turned sour and become embarrassing. He pokes fun, for example, at the way in which American boomers are customizing their own funeral services into a mixture of stand-up comedy and karaoke.

And Britain has not been immune to the backlash either. A

survey published in July 2006 discovered that many British baby-boomers are fibbing about their rebellious past: of the quarter who claimed to be hippies in the 1960s, for example, only 6 per cent actually were. While Bill Clinton might have pretended not to inhale, the sad truth is that most baby-boomers pretended that they did.

The self-hating boomer-bashers make interesting reading, but they do need to calm down and take a Valium. The problem with the generational blame-game is that it fails to do justice to the other things which motivate politics and social change. In any case, British baby-boomers do not have the same misplaced sense of generational solidarity as do their American cousins. Quite the opposite. The irony of communicating with the narcissistic British baby-boomers – as every advertiser already knows – is that many of them don't identify with their age group at all, but with someone twenty years younger.

Brand America

Whatever way you look at it, America's image in the world has never looked quite so bad. With no sign of a coherent exit strategy from its war in Iraq, things only seem to go from bad to worse for Brand America. Fear not, however, because some of America's brightest young graduates, toiling away in Madison Avenue advertising agencies, are working selflessly to stop the rot.

For the last fifty years, marketers of American brands were happy to ally themselves with the values of their home country –

Coca-Cola, Marlboro and Levi's were paraded as affordable slices of Americana – and consumers everywhere in the world took them at their word. In turn, those brands became willing ambassadors for the values which America wanted to portray as its own: liberty, for example, and material prosperity. Just recently, however, many big American brands have concluded that their homeland is as much of a hindrance as a help. Maybe it was the launch of Mecca-Cola in 2003, a soft drink aimed at cashing in on anti-American sentiment in the Middle East that finally put the breeze up Brand America. With the insulting tagline 'No more drinking stupid, drink with contentment', the ads for Mecca-Cola not only offended the marketers at Coca-Cola but also ruffled a few feathers at the US State Department.

Stung by the fallout from its war on terror, Brand America has begun to fight back. Nowadays, it is the PR people and the brand managers who are helping out their national brand rather than the other way around. Shortly after 11 September 2001, America launched the first TV advertising campaign for Brand America, broadcast to predominantly Muslim countries. In 2004, the Bush administration spent $685 million (about £380 million) on PR initiatives to promote America's flagging image abroad. The following year, President George Bush announced yet another campaign of public diplomacy: America was to become a *listening* brand. 'America's public diplomacy should be as much about listening and understanding as it is about speaking,' said the PR woman appointed by Mr Bush to head the campaign. 'I'm eager to listen and to learn.'

Whether the marketers can rescue Brand America is a moot point. In his book *Brand America: The Mother of All Brands* (2004), Simon Anholt offers a gloomy diagnosis. 'If Brand America slips far enough in people's esteem, there is a chance that American brands will one day have to work harder than others to downplay the negative associations of their country of origin. Or else, like so many brands from poor countries today ... they might need to conceal their country of origin.' Unless, that is, Brand America gets around to hiring him as a consultant.

Citizen Journalism

What a difference a sizeable terrorist outrage can make to the public image of camera phones? Until 7 July 2005, camera and video phones had been associated mainly with pop culture, prurience and paedophiles. In the aftermath of the calamitous terrorist attacks on London's transport system, however, all those perverts and nosy parkers suddenly morphed into intrepid 'citizen reporters'.

Changes in the media landscape only really become apparent in moments of extremity and, in the last couple of years, most countries have come face to face with their own dark epiphany about the power of the camera phone. The citizen snapper, armed with a camera phone or a hand-held digital camera, came of age in the UK after the suicide bombings of 7 July. Minutes after the bombings, newsrooms were being deluged with emailed pictures offering every conceivable perspective on the attacks. On the day of the bombs alone, the BBC received about 1,000 phone photos from the public. But citizen snappers are only one branch of the new amateur industry called 'citizen journalism'. In the last few years, different branches of the media industry have been forced into their own encounter with the amateurs as a hornet's nest of new digital and internet technologies has given rise to whisperings about a new kind of journalism – one whose distinctiveness lies in the fact that it is produced not by professionals but by amateur enthusiasts armed with no more than a computer, a camera phone, an internet connection, a digital camera or an iPod.

This idea of amateur newspaper reporting first surfaced in South Korea in 2000, when an online newspaper called *OhmyNews* had the inexpensive idea of soliciting most of its content from its readers. Launched with the slogan 'Every citizen is a reporter', the site has now been garlanded with awards for its originality. Then there arrived the citizen pundit, as the publication of running commentary on personal online weblogs evolved into a global cottage industry. By September 2007, there were 107 million blogs in the world; one champion of the new journalism imagines that, as a consequence of all this amateur activity, 'tomorrow's news reporting and production will be more of a conversation, or a seminar. The lines will blur between producers and consumers, changing the role of both in ways we're only beginning to grasp now.'

But are we really witnessing the birth of a new era of journalism, one in which the public collaborate with news outlets to report the news? One survey by the *American Online Journalism Review* suggests that blogs 'tend to be impressionistic, telegraphic, raw, honest, individualistic, highly opinionated and passionate, often striking an emotional chord'. The web of linkages which drive the internet and the blogosphere, however, can lend themselves to flurries of unsubstantiated rumour and malice. Without the relationship of trust between reporter and editor, how is anyone to authenticate what we are seeing through the grainy eye of a mobile phone? Unscrupulous news outlets, too, may use citizen reporters as an excuse to slacken the editorial process and penny-pinch on reporting budgets. And rubberneckers everywhere will have a convenient new call to arms – let me through, they'll cry, I'm a citizen reporter.

Compassion Fatigue

Every year, in one of Britain's more peculiar modern traditions, a whole evening's scheduling of BBC1 is given over to something called the Children in Need Appeal. Viewers are invited to sink deep into the sofa for an evening of watching minor celebrities doing embarrassing things with one other. It's all for charity, of course, and everyone is asked to dig deep.

Charity appeals like Children in Need seem to go from strength to strength every year, but they might well be drawing on a finite well of human compassion. The latest buzzword in the aid industry, 'compassion fatigue', refers to the psychological exhaustion said to be induced by endless appeals for money and sympathy. If charity begins at home, then compassion fatigue sets in when it reaches places far away. The head of the UN Development Programme, for example, has offered it as the explanation for the pathetic response to the humanitarian crisis following the earthquake in Pakistan and Kashmir in 2005. So debilitating has the new ailment become that the British

Department for International Development has launched a campaign aimed at tackling compassion fatigue by showing that small changes can make a big difference.

It is as though we have all been signed up to run the marathon for charity but find ourselves out of puff before we even reach the halfway mark. But it is not necessarily our fault. In her seminal 1999 book, *Compassion Fatigue*, the American academic Susan Moeller laid the blame at a very different door. 'Why,' she wonders, 'despite the haunting nature of many of these images, do we seem to care less and less about the world around us?' Moeller's answer was that the fickle glare of the media, rather than our innate selfishness, was to blame for our dwindling reserves of kindness. At least when it comes to international disasters, she argued, our compassion tends to be selective and framed by both fashion and the prevailing political and economic interests. Only after the Gulf War, for example, did the massacre of the Kurds at Halabja become headline news, because only then could it be squeezed into the prevailing categories of good versus bad.

Formulaic media coverage, Moeller argues, encourages us to be spectators at a pantomime of powerlessness. Images of starving children stare back at us and implore us to do something, emotions win out over analysis and within days the whole humanitarian circus has moved on and pitched up somewhere else. What starts with the noble aim of engaging our attention ends up numbing our senses and rendering us indifferent. If our consciences are full up, argues Moeller, it is only because of the mawkish pretend-compassion in which the media package bad news.

Perhaps we are suffering from an orgy of conspicuous caring rather than an overload of charitable requests. Big businesses, wealthy individuals and celebrities now compete with one another to show that they care. We can even outsource our consciences to corporations – buying Tesco vouchers for our local school, for instance. The business of giving is powdered with schmaltz and glamour and dressed up as entertainment. Maybe those homeless Pakistanis or destitute Africans simply do not exhibit enough gut-wrenching decrepitude, or enough pizzazz.

The Cosmetic Underclass

In his classic 1895 novel *The Time Machine*, H.G. Wells told the story of an inventor who teleported himself far into the distant future and was taken aback to discover that the human race had by then split into two different species, the Eloi and the Morlocks. The nice-but-dim Eloi lived a carefree life above ground, their only worry being the bestial, lumpen Morlocks who toiled all day long underground to keep them in the style to which they had become accustomed.

Wells's novel was a poisoned arrow aimed at the leisured class of unproductive toffs which he saw emerging in Edwardian England. Not for the first time, however, science fiction has subsequently been resurrected as scientific fact. At the end of 2006, for example, an evolutionary theorist at the London School of Economics called Oliver Curry announced that it was only a matter of time – 100,000 years in this case – before the human race split up into two different species: one genetically enhanced upper class and another coarse, ugly-looking underclass. The upper classes would be tall, healthy and intelligent, reckoned Curry, while the lower orders would all be ugly, goblin-like creatures – nasty, brutish, and rather short.

Stories like this, which imagine a future rift between genetic haves and have-nots, are beginning to find an echo in contemporary debates about the increased take-up of cosmetic surgery. Almost 700,000 cosmetic surgery operations, after all, will be performed in Britain this year at a cost of £ 539 million; by 2009, market analyst Mintel predicts, they are expected to top one million, at a cost of almost £ 1 billion. Many more are taking place abroad, with Spain becoming the cosmetic surgery centre of Europe. Large numbers of Brits, ostensibly on holiday there, are coming home with a new set of breasts and a wide-eyed pout which wouldn't look out of place on *Desperate Housewives*.

But are we really witnessing the birth of what some futurologists are calling a 'cosmetic underclass' – people who will, in the future, not be able to afford plastic surgery and will be forced to look their age as a result? It's an arresting idea, but there are reasons to be sceptical. Remember all that talk at the end of the last decade about an underclass of technological know-nothings whose inability to cross the chasm of the 'digital divide' was bound to hobble civil society for decades to come. It turns out that the so-called 'digital underclass' could well afford a computer and internet connection, but they didn't much see the point. The best argument against the emergence of a class of marauding uglies is that cosmetic surgery, a bit like computers and the net, is getting cheaper all the time. Very soon anyone will be able to afford it and – as a consequence – it might become as tacky as a fake tan.

Cosmopolitanism

Nearly 200 million people now live outside their country of origin, according to a recent United Nations survey, a figure that has leapt up by a staggering 25 per cent since 1990. New technology and mass migration are helping to make the world a much smaller place, but we persist in thinking of ourselves as more different from each other than ever. Drafted in to help solve this anomaly, the notion of cosmopolitanism is making a spectacular intellectual comeback.

Cosmopolitanism dates from Greek society in the fourth century BC, where a 'cosmopolitan' was said to be a citizen of the world, or someone whose loyalties transcended a particular state or polity. Later on, it was borrowed by some philosophers of the European Enlightenment to help define the universal rights of man. After both Hitler and Stalin had inveighed against untrustworthy 'rootless cosmopolitans' in the twentieth century, however, the idea fell into disuse. Kwame Anthony Appiah, raised in Ghana, educated in Britain and now a Professor of Moral Philosophy at Princeton, might be the ideal standard-bearer to help revive it. In his elegant new book *Cosmopolitanism: Ethics in a World of Strangers* (2006), Appiah joins several of the world's leading thinkers – Martha Nussbaum, Amartya Sen and Ulrich Beck – who have recently railed against the dangers of cultural isolationism.

Cosmopolitanism, according to Appiah, should nowadays be thought of as the welding together of two very different principles: that we owe obligations to other human beings beyond those we are related to by ties of national citizenship, but also that we have an obligation to take seriously the ways in which people in different cultures choose to live. Unlike the Ancient Greeks, he points out, we can now be citizens of the world in a real sense because the cultural miscegenation that goes with mass migration constantly frays the ropes tethering us to a national culture. Saudis, for example, can now watch Western sitcoms on satellite television, knowing that the behaviours laughed off by their characters might result in public beheading in their own country.

Appiah is good at demolishing the rhetoric of those who seem to enforce diversity, and who, as a result, risk trapping people within differences they might prefer to avoid. Patronizing talk about the inviolability of different cultures, he says, 'now just amounts to telling other people what they ought to value in their own traditions'. He advocates deliberately contaminating cultures with new influences whether they like it or not. Cultures so fragile that they cannot withstand contamination, he implies, hardly deserve our protection.

Any defence of cosmopolitanism, however, is going to be a high-wire act. Appiah is trying to balance our local loyalties with our global responsibilities, trying to emphasize our common humanity without shoehorning us into a shared morality. Where he falls short is in his inability to give substance or impetus to our global humanity beyond occasional acts of charity or intervention in humanitarian emergencies. We must not insist that everyone become cosmopolitan, he says – which makes it sound more of a dandyish intellectual proposition than a practical political idea. His cosmopolitan refusal to be pinned down on the values that underpin his global community leaves him looking a little, well, rootless.

Crowd-Sourcing

Are the best decisions always made by a single sage, or by a tiny clique of wise men? James Surowiecki thinks the answer is neither. In his influential book, *The Wisdom of Crowds*, this staff writer on the *New Yorker* magazine argues that decisions taken by large groups are almost always better than those of small numbers of experts – even when those in the large group aren't very bright. This apparently simple thesis, he argues, has profound implications for how businesses, organizations and nation-states operate. Consider, for example, the recent success of so-called 'decision markets', in which enthusiastic amateurs bet on the prospects of celebrities and politicians. They include Iowa Electronic Markets, a scheme set up to let people place bets on, amongst other things, how they think political candidates will perform in future elections. Information markets like these work, says Surowiecki, because the incentive to do better than others makes everyone into sleuths, and the absence of any hierarchy prevents them from swallowing uncomfortable opinions. The same logic helps explain why stock markets are so good at allocating capital, and why contestants on *Who Wants to be a Millionaire?* are usually better off asking the audience than phoning a friend.

Harnessing the wisdom of crowds has come to be known as crowd-sourcing, and now everyone is at it. But the concept is not entirely convincing. What about the popular delusions that now drive crowds to irrational ends, such as the collective mania that seemed to overcome many investors at the height of the internet boom? Surowiecki counters that his notion of collective wisdom only works when aggregating thousands of decisions arrived at independently; collective wisdom can only manifest itself when the judgements of each individual were arrived at independently and then totted up at the end. Where decisions cease to be properly independent of each other, such as when continuous TV coverage of the dot.com economy led everyone up the same blind alley, his hypothesis can no longer hold.

So when exactly does his thesis hold good? Surowiecki assesses the accuracy of internet-based 'decision markets' in which members of the public are invited to take bets on the career prospects of celebrities and politicians. He is particularly enamoured with the Policy Analysis Market (PAM), a short-lived initiative dreamed up by boffins at the US Defense Department in 2003, that encouraged the public to bet on future terrorist calamities in the hope they might do better than the experts. Such was the elegance of his promise that it was soon being borrowed by supporters of voluntary online projects like Wikipedia. The collective judgement arrived at by harnessing the aggregate intelligence of millions, argued devotees of the Wiki, could make for a far more efficient and responsive reference tool than its competitors. Even the toy company Lego, for example, now uses crowd-sourcing to let visitors to its website design Lego models and upload them to a gallery to show off their skills. It recently inaugurated a contest in which the winning ten models were sold as Lego models, with the creators earning 5 per cent of the revenues.

The humbling of Wikipedia – since 2005, there have been several noisy scandals about its reliability – helps us to put the alleged wisdom of crowds in perspective. Crowd-sourcing can be insightful, but only in limited situations, for example, when new ideas or suggestions are badly needed, or when the only alternative is guesswork. Rather like the ranking of results on Google,

Wikipedia is best seen as a global memory bank or conversation – an imperfect stream of consciousness which is constantly updating itself and making fruitful connections, but which is also susceptible to rumour and jitteriness, partisanship and old-fashioned rigging. Immerse yourself in the wisdom of these lonely crowds by all means, but rely on it at your peril.

Crunchy Conservatism

When David Cameron set out on his long media march to modernize the Conservative party, he could have done with a look at the idea of 'crunchy conservatism'. Crunchy conservatism sounds like a new breakfast cereal, but in these marketing-friendly times that might be no bad thing. It began life in the United States a few years back, when Rod Dreher, a journalist at the conservative *National Review*, mentioned to his colleagues that he was off to shop for organic vegetables and became the office laughing-stock. Emboldened by the experience to clarify his political beliefs, Dreher wrote a series of articles and then a book making an impassioned plea for a return to an old-fashioned, anti-modern variety of conservatism.

Crunchy conservativism, according to Dreher, is a sensibility as much as a political movement. Crunchy conservatives are as anti-consumerist and as sceptical about big business as the left; they detest suburban sprawl, shopping malls, fast-food eateries, and all the other detritus of the consumer society. They distinguish themselves from hippies of the left, he says, because they are more interested in beauty and aesthetics, and more suspicious of the power of the state. Rather than invoke regulation, the crunchies seek to lead by example. The Dreher household, he proudly tells us, rarely watches any television and makes its own muesli and apple butter.

Dreher is too much of a God-botherer for British tastes, and a little too uptight, but otherwise his insistence that there is more to life than money echoes Cameron's campaign. Crunchy conservatists thinks they can answer the question that the market cannot – how we can enjoy our wealth once we have made it. And, like Cameron, who has admitted cycling to work followed by a government car to carry his briefcase, the crunchy conservative cares as much about aesthetics as about the environment.

Crunchy conservatism comes with a distinguished pedigree. Only since the 1970s, it is often forgotten, has environmentalism been associated with the left. Before that, Dreher's quixotic approach would have seen him pigeonholed as a remnant of the fading aristocratic elite, those responsible stewards of the land with servants who prepared their organic meals. Even now, a hand-to-mouth existence is most elegantly achieved with the help of a silver spoon. In Britain, a list of leading crunchy conservatives would include Zac Goldsmith, Jonathan Porritt and Prince Charles – toffs of the highest calibre, and all keen to conserve the land in the most traditional sense.

The role models and paraphernalia associated with crunchy conservatism might sound a little antediluvian, but these can surely be tinkered with by Cameron in focus groups at a later date. An alliance of cyclists, joggers and dog-walkers might not sound very promising, but there are a good many of them about.

Curation Nation

At the beginning of 2006, the grandly titled British Association of Aesthetic Plastic Surgeons announced that the number of operations carried out under its auspices had soared by 35 per cent on the previous year's figures. The middle classes, it gloated, are basking in the new 'cultural permission' to plump for plastic or cosmetic surgery. Let's hope they look good.

Cosmetic surgery has traditionally been criticized by feminists, but many of those operations will have been carried out on teenagers or young women, and most of them do not care a fig about the moral strictures of feminism. They are more likely to think of cosmetic surgery as an aesthetic modification of their bodies, a positive and empowering lifestyle choice. Body modification through plastic surgery, however, is only one aspect of a more general vogue for transforming and manipulating everything we can call our own. Young people do it best and, as everything migrates into the digital world, teenagers are quietly becoming expert at modifying everything that falls into their laps. A recent survey by the American Pew Research Center found that nearly one in five American teenagers don't simply steal video or images from the worldwide web but rejig them into something distinctively their own – adding their own ending for the latest *Star Wars* film, for example, or reworking their favourite novel or cult TV show.

In North America, futurologists have begun to dub this fetish for branding our bodies and our immediate surroundings as 'curation nation' – a world in which we have all become artists and curators of the minutiae of our own lives, capable of sampling, editing, or cutting and pasting anything that crosses our path. For at least a decade, most future-gazers have been entertaining audiences with the prediction that mass culture will give way to a world of 'mass customization' – in which everything from the trainers we wear to the cars we drive will be tailored to our own specification and made to measure by companies with access to swanky new technologies. That prediction has stubbornly failed to materialize, but now, as young people get their hands on the technology, it is slowly coming true – not in the things we buy but in the bodies we inhabit.

This culture of endless customization is better understood as a cultural rather than a technological phenomenon, and is darker than its promoters imagine. Another recent survey estimated that a million British adolescents have considered self-harm and more than 800,000 actually inflicted injuries on themselves. Many will see themselves as curators or artists, etching out something of beauty on the only thing they really control. They may even be right. But the real problem – much more hair-raising than a routine facelift – is that many young people are turning inwards in search of inspiration, and have given up the chance to paint on a broader canvas.

The Cyborg

Cyberspace is dead, says one of its leading gurus William J. Mitchell, and long live the cyborg. The notion of cyberspace is usually credited to the American novelist William Gibson, who wrote about it more than twenty years ago. It is a wholly fantastical notion when you stop to think about it – the idea that, a little like Harry Potter, we can slip away into an infinite netherworld hidden within the cables connecting up all the computers in the world.

Metaphors such as these might have been good enough when we were struggling to understand this new electronic connecting machine but, according to Mitchell (now the head of the Media Lab at the super-futuristic Massachusetts Institute of Technology), they have long outlived their usefulness. Mitchell's book, *ME+ +*, is an attempt to fill in the gaps, to understand the effects of all this on our already media-savvy selves at a time when digital access to the web and to each other is so commonplace as to have become a utility like gas or water. His argument is that, with the advent of mobile devices and wireless internet access, digital bits no longer exist in a separate sphere called cyberspace but have gone on location in the real world. Whereas much of what goes on to the worldwide web is cocooned in the parallel universe of cyberspace, Mitchell says, new wireless technologies such as mobile phones and location-positioning technology are creating a more harmonious marriage between the virtual and the real. 'The trial separation of bits and atoms is now over,' he announces at the beginning of his book. 'Routinely, events in cyberspace are being reflected in physical space, and vice versa.' The result, he claims, is the rise of a human cyborg, 'a biological core surrounded by extended, constructed systems of boundaries and networks'. The social ties that exist in this new world 'are no longer provided by a contiguous home turf; increasingly, my sense of continuity and belonging derives from being electronically networked to the widely scattered people and places I care about'.

Today's handheld wireless devices, says Mitchell, are held so indispensably close to our bodies that they have got under our skins. Further, the network of wireless connections between ourselves, other people and our surroundings is transforming how we navigate our way around the city. Almost invisibly, we have all turned into cyborgs or 'electronomads' (human bodies with embedded digital extensions) and have the city as our network. A world governed less by physical boundaries and more by an ongoing engagement between the digital and the real will make life more exciting, according to Mitchell. The city will become a metaphorical body, with the blood of its citizens pulsating through its veins at breakneck speed.

Mitchell looks forward to a future in which we will be able to implant in our teeth silicon chips for identification, memory tags to store our medical records, even wireless speakers for our mobile telephones (thus eliminating the need for any of that embarrassing 'hands-free' equipment). There exists the possibility 'to change the fundamental mechanics of reference – the ways in which we establish meaning, construct knowledge, and make sense of our surroundings by associating items of information with one another and with physical objects'. He concludes his paean to digital modernism by arguing that the cities of the twenty-first century will be defined not by stone fortifications, nor by boundaries drawn on today's political maps, but by 'the endless hum of electromagnetic variations'. The brave new world of the cyborg will also allow us to rethink urban life from the bottom up, presenting opportunities for innovation among architects, town planners and employers – and, presumably, putting sci-fi writers out of a job.

Declinology

In 2006 China officially leapfrogged both Britain and France to become the world's fourth biggest economy, giving doomsayers in both European countries a fresh opportunity to wring their hands in ritual despair. As fading former colonial powers, both the French and the British have made revelling in their own decline into a national pastime. In Britain, some of the most sought-after books of recent years have included *Talk to the Hand* (2005), Lynne Truss's hissy whinge about the decline of good manners, and *Is It Just Me or Is Everything Shit?* (2005), a diatribe penned by a couple of overgrown schoolboys who don't like anything that's been invented since the CD made its appearance.

At least the French can claim to whinge with a little élan. There, rueing the fact that everything is going down the tubes is an intellectual as well as a trivial pursuit. The determination of its novelists to paint a gloomy picture of French society, for example, has been labelled by the critics as a mood of *déprimisme*, or *depressivism*. At the head of that movement is Michel Houellebecq, the literary shock-jock whose pornographic predictions of human catastrophe get progressively more fantastical with every book he writes. Now the intellectuals have their own movement: declinology.

'I see the appearance of a new population in our country, the new experts: declinologists,' the former French Prime Minister Dominique de Villepin recently declared. Former President Jacques Chirac waded in too, blaming intellectuals for their 'permanent self-flagellation'. It's true that the French love to castigate themselves, and that they enjoy nothing more than a good crisis. Otherwise they would have little conversation to punctuate those long lunches and meandering family dinners. But what do they have to be melancholic about? Riots in the suburbs, to be sure, and the slow decline of Paris as a literary melting pot. But that is not the whole story. At the same time that they are supposedly drowning in melancholia, *The Economist* reports a survey that suggests that 84 per cent of French people are quite content with their lot.

There is a curious paradox here, and one that has been troubling European economists and sociologists for some years. Griping, doom-mongering and general wailing about the state of things are hardly novel, and are as likely to come from critics on the right as on the left. But in survey after survey in recent years, the same people who purport to believe that society is going to hell in a handcart are liable to add that their own circumstances have never been better. One such survey identifies Europeans as 'egoptimists' – adamant that their quality of life and finances are rosy, but equally convinced that society is going down the tubes.

How are we to explain the anomaly? Maybe it is an illusion fostered by mortgages, pensions and insurance products that we can insulate ourselves from the fortunes of the rest of society. But the paradox extends into culture, too – our literary sensibilities can hardly be in such disrepute when Houellebecq's weighty philosophical novels are on so many of our shelves. Declinology turns out to be a rather antisocial complaint: not everything has gone to hell, just everyone else. Translated into English, that means that everything is shit except you.

Democratization

Democratization is an ugly word, bearing about as much relationship to real democracy as a forced marriage does to romantic love. The idea was the brainchild of political scientists and lawyers, who used it to describe the way that successive waves of countries emerged from authoritarianism to liberal democracy during the post-war period and the constitutional alternatives available to help them on their way.

At the beginning of the twenty-first century, however, it was press-ganged into service by the US government. The argument of the neoconservatives who surround the Republican administration – and one that occasionally puts in an appearance in the speeches of George Bush – was that planting the seeds of democracy in the Middle East might make the place more resistant to virulent strains of Islamist extremism. Amidst the bedlam of Iraq, that theory is now mounting a hasty retreat. Writing in the prestigious American journal *Foreign Affairs*, for example, F. Gregory Gause III, Professor of Political Science at the University of Vermont, argues that there is no empirical evidence to suggest that democracy snuffs out terrorism.

Far from it, he argues. Between 1976 and 2004, Gause produces statistics to show that there were 400 terrorist incidents in democratic India and only eighteen in non-democratic China. There is, Gause concludes in his survey, 'no solid empirical evidence for a strong link between democracy, or any other regime type, and terrorism, in either a positive or a negative direction'. The problem is that democracy is inherently destabilizing – if it were a technology, it might be called disruptive – which is why ruling elites have

x

traditionally tried to keep it under control. The most democratic decade in Britain of the previous half-century was probably the 1970s, but few of us want to return there anytime soon.

The situation is doubly fraught in Iraq, where there are fledgling democratic institutions but little evidence of any real enthusiasm for popular sovereignty or nationhood. The transitions to democracy that we are familiar with – from Spain in the mid-1970s to South Africa in the early 1990s – were, at least in part, responses to the will of the people. Unlike previous 'waves of democratization', however, this new one has been conceived from without and in strictly instrumental terms – not as a good in itself, but because it might open up a more benign kind of politics in the Middle East and help marginalize Islamist extremism.

The Bush administration is now in a bind. If it backtracks on its democratizing mission in Iraq and throws in its lot with a local Iraqi strongman – and there are plenty to choose from – it will be accused of toppling Saddam in favour of a kind of Saddam-lite. But if it presses ahead with its attempts at democratization, it seems likely to end up with a bastard democracy whose very shapelessness invites sectarian rivalries and offers a red rag to the terrorists who want to provoke it into revealing its authoritarian colours. Whichever direction its takes, America's wave of democratization has already slowed into a trickle, and may already have gone into reverse.

Digital Maoism

Cheerleaders for the idea of the wisdom of crowds should be tied to a chair and forced to sit through that terrifyingly awful film blockbuster called *Snakes on a Plane*. The script had reportedly been given the thumbs-down by thirty different studios before a mention of it on a blog ignited a flurry of interest and numerous suggestions, some of which made their way into the finished version. Not only was *Snakes on a Plane* hyped into existence on the web; it can claim to be the first movie whose production tapped into the decentralized collective intelligence that is freely available online. So popular has this knowingly execrable film become that its title has passed into popular slang to mean a world-weary shrug – a twenty-first-century version of 'such is life'.

Snakes on a Plane is hardly the best example of what collective endeavour on the web can achieve, but it should be enough to send a shiver up the spine all the same. It arrived at the same time as a minor backlash against the merits of 'social intelligence' or 'online collectivism'. In his 2006 essay 'Digital Maoism: The Hazards to the New Online Collectivism', posted in the intellectual online review *Edge*, Jaron Lanier has thrown a Molotov cocktail at the idea that collective intelligence is worth getting excited about. Lanier has no problem with unfolding experiments in online intelligence like the do-it-yourself encyclopedia Wikipedia. His beef is with how these experiments in the 'hive mind' have been turned into oracles overnight. Our understandable enthusiasm for new variations on collective action, Lanier suggests, has made the web into an almost metaphysical entity – a headless, formless, agglomerate monster, prone to ill-considered flurries of enthusiasm, and irrational and sometimes dangerous stampedes.

Just as technologists used to bend over backwards to look dumb so as to make artificially intelligent computers look smart, Lanier argues that we now fawn over and patronize the new internet collectivism to make it look smarter than it really is. 'If we start to believe the internet itself is an entity that has something to say,' says Lanier, 'we're devaluing those people and making ourselves into idiots.'

The online collective isn't always stupid. The blogosphere can correct the failings and inaccuracies of the broadcast media, as it did recently when it pounced on a freelance Reuters photographer accused of doctoring pictures of the aftermath of an Israeli bombing raid on Beirut. The moral of Lanier's story is that sometimes this kind of collective intelligence yields results and sometimes it doesn't. It is more likely to be clever, he claims, when it isn't defining its own questions, when the answer can be reduced to a simple numeric value and when there is a quality-control mechanism or feedback loop that relies on individual initiative. Break any of those conditions, he says, and the 'hive mind' is likely to be worse than useless, or to spin wildly out of control. The good news is that, from now on, anyone ambushed by a cock-up in the collective intelligence will have an easy refrain – don't worry about it, buddy, snakes on a plane.

Digital Mapping

Little phones you carry in your pocket which use satellite-tracking technology to pinpoint your location to just a few centimetres; itty-bitty tags which supermarkets use to track their products; bus passes which simultaneously monitor your body temperature to find out how often you're having sex ...

OK, so I dropped in the last one to perk things up a little. But am I alone in suppressing a yawn every time I hear a scary tabloid-style investigation into the perils of our 'surveillance society'? Privacy campaigners are quite right that we need to keep an eye on our civil liberties, but in the hands of newspaper hacks their arguments have become blunt and stale; when they're not bludgeoning us with gobbledygook about technology, they're hamming it up by implying some sinister conspiracy in which our every movement is being monitored. Part of you wants to pat them on the back, but secretly you're getting bored and turning the page, and thinking it might be a lost cause anyway.

One of the problems with the 'surveillance society' rhetoric is that it loses sight of how new technology might be put to good use. Take the project currently underway at the Media Lab at the Massachusetts Institute of Technology. For some years now, researchers there have been working on an ambitious experiment in Rome to use the data from people's mobile phones, along with GPS devices mounted on taxis and buses, to create a dynamic tracking tool capable of producing a real-time map of how the city is used by its citizens. The MIT project created quite a stir when it was launched at the Venice Biennale of 2006 as a project called 'Real Time Rome'. If it became widely available, this kind of digital mapping could be used to alleviate congestion of traffic or people. In time, however, it could also become a goldmine for architects, urban planners and designers who want to build better cities – or even for artists, who want to intervene in the urban landscape.

The possibilities are endless, but only if we overcome our paranoia about surveillance and put proper controls on how we use such information. To do so is perfectly possible: the MIT project, for example, uses data which has been stripped of any details that might identify anyone personally. Sometimes, however, we might want to know exactly what is under surveillance. At the beginning of September, it was reported that a Canadian non-governmental organization (NGO) had used digital mapping technology to prove that a good deal of Peruvian coffee which is slapped with the 'ethical' or 'fair trade' label is nothing of the sort. The moral? Be suspicious of tracking devices by all means – but everything depends on who is being tracked, why and who by.

The Economy of Prestige

Scarcely a week goes by without another gong-giving avalanche of plaudits being thrust upon us. Prize-giving has reached such a frenzy that 2004 saw the inauguration of the Awards awards, an opportunity for the great and good in the British awards industry to slap each other on the back and indulge in some saccharine speeches of their own. What could possibly be wrong with giving out a few gongs? Plenty, according to a new book, *The Economy of Prestige*, by an American academic called James F. English. The remarkable ascendancy of prizes in literature and the arts over the last century, according to English, 'is one of the great untold stories of modern cultural life'. No ambitious CV is now complete without a smattering of obscure prizes and recondite awards. British writers can now compete for about 300 prizes. The number of film awards distributed each year is now more than the number of full-length films being made. Prizes are big business. The annual expenditure on the annual Orange Prize for Fiction in terms of promotions and book club tie-ins, for example, exceeds the value of the prize itself by about ten times.

In the economy of prestige, even supposedly worthy prizes descend into self-parody and become cultural entertainment in their own right, as the ribaldry at the annual British Press Awards eloquently testifies. The yearly flurry of scandal, mischief-making, gossip and bitchiness that surrounds the Booker or the Turner Prize have become their lifeblood, as all of those involved in it seem instinctively to understand. Pouring scorn on these glittering prizes merely feeds their publicity machine. 'It is the charge of fundamental, irremediable illegitimacy,' says English, 'that keeps a prize a focus of attention.'

Booby prizes or anti-prizes such as that annual bacchanal, The Bad Sex in Fiction awards, are part of the same phenomenon, says English, as they only attempt to measure according to an alternative scale of cultural value. The growth of anti-prizes, he argues, are signs not of the exhaustion of the prize-giving bonanza but of its infinite flexibility – defining what is bad, after all, is just as telling a cultural judgement as any best-in-show prize. In any case, the difference between prizes and anti-prizes has become blurred. When the K Foundation poked fun at the Turner Prize in 1994 by announcing a prize of its own for Worst British Artist, a number of artists phoned in to demand that their work be entered in the new competition.

Prizes have become so crucial a cultural institution that the excellence they are supposed to reward can easily be drowned out in the drumroll. English's conclusion is that in our republic of entertainment, 'the seriousness of prizes has been eroded without any corresponding erosion of their efficacy.' But effective for whom? It would be tempting to say that there are no prizes for guessing. But there probably are.

Electronic Frontier Justice

The campaign to tame the Wild West of the virtual world goes on, but the outlaws continue to claim scalps. Take Kaavya Viswanathan, a nineteen-year-old Harvard undergraduate who had struck a book deal worth a reputed half a million dollars. At the beginning of May 2006 Viswanathan came unstuck when it emerged that whole chunks of her debut novel had been cribbed from another writer. The initial allegations surfaced in a Harvard newspaper, but very soon they had been sucked into the blogosphere; with many internet eyes on her work, other offences were soon added to the charge sheet and her literary death warrant was signed. The book was pulped and its author shamed.

The New York Times dubbed it an example of 'frontier justice', but at least this time the inhabitants of the web were on the side of the just. As the internet makes it so much easier to transport and manipulate creative material, it has long stood accused of being a charter for plagiarists. For students with a deadline, its temptations are manifold – some prefer to order up bespoke essays from shady websites, while many prefer to cut and paste fragments of text into a final product that they can call their own. It is also a gold mine for novelists in search of a story. Giving evidence about his working methods in the unsuccessful plagiarism suit against him in March 2006, the novelist and amateur theologian Dan Brown admitted to using tall stories from the web, downloaded by his wife, as inspiration for his book *The Da Vinci Code*.

Slowly, however, the tables are turning. The vast quarries of resources on the web heighten the temptation to steal, but they also make theft easier to detect. Teachers now dip random phrases from suspiciously erudite student essays into Google to ensure that the work they are handed has had no previous owners. Sophisticated software packages and search databases are being touted around to help detect literary theft. Had her publishers invested in one, Viswanathan's borrowings would surely have been picked up earlier in the production chain.

The best kind of detection, however, is a human alarm system. The web lends itself to flurries of unsubstantiated rumour and malice, but it is also an excellent way of holding plagiarists to account. Ever since literary criticism expanded to include online chatter, writers have been on their guard against the piranhas of the web, who feast on every inaccuracy and gang up shamelessly for the kill. Neither are they afraid of meting out justice to one another. A conservative blogger hired by the *Washington Post* was quickly given the boot by the paper after a lynch mob of determined liberal bloggers discovered that some of his earlier writing was borrowed from the work of others.

Before the bloggers get too big for their boots, however, they need to reflect on their own predicament. Blogging works best when it is endlessly malleable and open to modification – much of what bloggers do consists of cutting, pasting and twisting the work of professional journalists into interesting new shapes. The same goes for the kind of videos aired on sites such as YouTube. com, many of which are mainstream films mashed up into exciting new forms. Lay down the law on all of this and you risk wading into a swamp of disputes about context and ownership. The collaborative ethic of the net is built around stealing of a kind; those who benefit from lawlessness should think twice before setting themselves up as sheriff.

The European Empire

The European Union is on an eastward roll and gobbling up every-thing before it. Until a few years back, it was a little club of fifteen countries in Western Europe. As a result of its popularity, it now has twenty-five members, with Bulgaria and Romania – subject to a few conditions – due to join in 2007.

The expanded European Union generates about a quarter of the world's GDP and more than a fifth of global trade. It is already the biggest economic bloc in the world and the largest single market. But just what is it? For decades now, political scientists have struggled to do conceptual justice to the organization's many-layered web of overlapping jurisdictions. It can't be a union of completely sovereign states, as its constituent countries have signed away some of that sovereignty as a condition of joining up. But it can't be a European super-state either, as its centre is so shaky and its lack of democratic legitimacy so stark. Not for nothing did Jacques Delors once call it an 'unidentified political object'.

In his new book *Europe as Empire*, the Oxford academic Jan Zielonka has come up with a novel solution to the problem. Europe, he cheekily suggests, is best characterized not as a state at all but as a hulking great imperial juggernaut, moving slowly but determinedly east and south. While intellectuals in Western Europe sniff that the EU's expansion might be incompatible with its underlying values, and those in the east fume against it as a harbinger of decadence and moral decline, Dr Zielonka suggests both are looking at the matter the wrong way around. The wave of enlargement that followed the fall of communism not only made the EU bigger, he argues, but fundamentally changed the character of the union.

Unlike the nation-state, Zielonka points out, the EU is not rooted in any particular territory or homeland and does not see its existing borders as set in stone. Its expansion eastwards is no more than an astute act of foreign policy by an empire on the rise: faced with potential instability at its margins, it simply overran itself and swallowed the problem. Many more countries, he points out, are hovering on the margins of the EU and waiting to be digested when the time is right. The EU, he notices, has become closely involved in the affairs of the fledgling Palestinian state. Israel, Lebanon and Jordan are all culturally close to Europe, and might also be tempted to join. Many in Ukraine, too, are warming to EU membership. And if Ukraine joins, what is to stop the EU from reaching as far as Belarus, or even Russia itself?

Dr Zielonka sees the expansion of the European empire as essentially benign. Labelling the EU's mission as an imperial one, however, is not enough to solve the problem of its lack of legitimacy. Dr Zielonka is too easily pleased. He gets excited about 'hybrid multilevel European governance in concentric circles' – a long way from bringing the EU closer to the people and hardly a slogan that is likely to catch on. Without firm roots, the problem with empires, even benign ones, is that they tend to overreach themselves and collapse from within.

The Experience Economy

Which would you prefer – to own a Ferrari or to take time out to walk the Machu Picchu trail in southern Peru? More and more of us, it seems, would prefer to take the walk. The elusive route to contentment, according to one of the most influential business theories of the last decade, lies not in material possessions but in experiences such as scuba-diving and exotic holidays.

The idea of the experience economy was first articulated in 1998, in a long article in the *Harvard Business Review* by the business guru James Gilmore. Jaded by the treadmill accumulation of goods and services, Gilmore argued, people are increasingly blowing their money on experiences instead. The next competitive battleground, he predicted, would lie in staging sensuous experiences with which to wow and seduce the consumer. Companies of all kinds must become like theatre directors, using the goods and services that they want to sell as props for a memorable event. Walt Disney's theme parks were held up as the way forward; in Disneyland, the workers are called actors, visitors are guests and the theme park becomes a stage.

Gilmore's thesis was the economics of the fun house, but it caught on all the same. It explains why brands like Nike, threatened with having their retail operation eclipsed by the internet, transformed their stores into glitzy retail experiences so that punters would spend more time and money in them. The idea of the experience economy explains why your local bookstore has added a coffee bar, to encourage its customers to stick around and browse. It explains why grocery stores began piping baking smells around the store to add a little frisson to the experience of buying a loaf; why small businesses emerged to indulge those who enjoy spending their birthday being hurled out of an aeroplane, or driving a tank around rural Ukraine; even why museums and art galleries began to jazz up their exhibits by dressing them up as interactive experiences.

But what good is an experience? According to the theory, experiences are valued because memories last longer than material goods, which are prone to wear and tear. They are also unique. The Joneses next door might have the same Ferrari as I do, but they are unlikely to have taken a year off to drive a converted shopping trolley around rural China. But the problem with selling experiences is that they can be miserable and dull as well as thrilling. And as we splurge more and more on expensive experiences, they begin to look like measurable commodities too

– chosen not for their intrinsic worth but because we can brag about them afterwards. An experience, it turns out, can be as much an instrument of social competition and one-upmanship as a sports car. Are you experienced? If so, you'd be doing everyone a favour if you kept it to yourself.

The Free Rider
or Collective Action Problem
and the Prisoner's Dilemma

The prisoner's dilemma game – sometimes known as the collective action problem or the free rider problem – is probably the most important and most intractable intellectual puzzle of the last hundred years, and one that has troubled the best mathematicians and social scientists of the modern era. It points up a conflict between what is rational for everyone in a given group to want collectively and what is rational for each individual within that group to do about it. Where there is a collective good that would benefit everyone in a certain group, its logic suggests, it will always be in the interest of each member of that group to free-ride – to benefit from that good without contributing to its provision.

In its modern form, the free rider concept was devised by two psychologists working for the American military think tank the RAND Corporation in 1950, one of a number of suspect strategic ideas whose purpose was to help America win its game of nuclear brinkmanship with the Soviet Union. Very soon, however, it began to spread its wings to become the dominant paradigm in the social sciences. Since then, it has been used by academics and politicians to help explain how much money government should spend on our behalf, to investigate how pressure groups take control of the political process, and even to explain our neglect of the environment. In the 1960s, the model was invoked by the libertarian right to explain why pressure groups are not usually joined by those they claim to represent. A decade later, it was being used by social-democratic economists to argue that there were strict logical limits to the benefits that could be had from economic growth.

By 1980, in a laughably desperate attempt to solve the free rider problem, an American social scientist called Robert Axelrod was attempting to find a solution to the problem by hooking up hundreds of powerful computers and having them repeatedly play each other in a bizarre tournament. By the end of the decade, the collective action problem had even expanded its empire into the natural sciences, where its enthusiasts claimed – not wholly convincingly – that it could help explain human evolution. In the real world, meanwhile, collective action as manifested in Western welfare states was in full retreat.

Study it carefully, because the free rider or collective action problem is not as simple or as innocent as it looks, and is as much of an ideological plaything as a logical puzzle. Understand its dimensions, however, and you begin to see it all around you. Nowadays, some of our most politically charged debates are over environmental problems such as traffic congestion, over-fishing and global warming. But as soon as we accept the diagnosis of the environmentalists, the voluntary collective activity that is

43

required to take remedial action to deal with these problems falls prey to the temptation for individuals to take a free ride. Can you think of a way to resolve this problem?

Futurology

Forecasting the future is a perilous business, but one which, at the beginning of the twenty-first century, has never been healthier. Such is our anxiety about the future that nowadays almost every large organization comes with its own futurologist or trends guru. Very rarely, however, does anyone measure the performance of these paid seers. By the time their prognostications have resolutely failed to materialize, most of us have forgotten all about them.

Until now, that is. Twenty years ago, an American psychologist called Philip Tetlock worked himself up into a rage at how rarely pundits ever admitted the errors in their predictions. Setting himself up as an honest broker and industry referee, Tetlock picked 284 people – academics, economists, journalists and policy wonks – who made their living hawking advice on political and economic trends, and asked them for testable predictions about the future. The results of his study are now in, and they make sobering reading. In over 300 pages of his book, *Expert Political Judgment: How Good Is It? How Can We Know?* Tetlock demonstrates in meticulous academic detail that most expert forecasters are no better than the rest of us at the prognostication game. Worse, when he informed them that they had been rumbled, most refused to eat humble pie and instead claimed to have been right all along.

What can be done about the future-fibbers? Part of the problem is the lack of transparency and rigour within the profession. Futurology is a bastard discipline, a synthesis of a wide variety of subjects. Anyone can set up shop in it, with the result that most of its practitioners know very little about anything. Built into the discipline, too, is a tendency towards hyberbole and exaggerating the new. Those forecasters who pull from the bag startlingly counter-intuitive predictions win cachet and kudos, while those who predict the blindingly obvious can expect to be back in the dole queue before very long.

Tetlock concludes with an appeal for humility. 'We as a society,' he says, 'would be better off if participants in policy debates stated their beliefs in testable forms, monitored their forecasting performance, and honored reputational bets.' For the career futurologist, however, the moral of the story might be to make parsimonious and rather nebulous prognostications, and to sit on the fence wherever possible. Writing to Friedrich Engels in 1857 about a risky punt he had taken on the progress of a political rebellion in India, Karl Marx gave solid advice. 'It's possible,' he admitted, 'that I shall make an ass of myself. But in that case one can always get out of it with a little dialectic. I have, of course, so worded my proposition as to be right either way.' Ambitious forecasters take note.

Generation Gap

Whatever happens at the next British general election, David Cameron has given the Conservative party the makeover of a lifetime. Whether he is seen riding along on a bicycle, skating in the Arctic or admiring the wind turbines on his house, all of his efforts have been designed to outflank New Labour on its home turf of social conscience. Most of it conforms to a masterplan to win back the affections of 'Generation Gap'.

A former PR man for a television company, David Cameron knows a thing or two about how to slice up an audience into different marketing demographics. 'Generation Gap', or 'the wristband generation', is the latest demographic acronym to emerge from the bowels of our marketing-friendly modern political machine. Even before Cameron won the leadership campaign, in a pamphlet called *True Blue: How Fair Conservatism can win the next election*, published by the London think tank Demos, Nicholas Boys Smith, a Conservative party strategist and a confidant of Cameron's inner circle, set out the new strategy.

Boys Smith first twigged that something was amiss when, while chin-wagging with his peers at Cambridge University, he began to be embarrassed by his Conservative affiliations. Generation Gap, he argues in his pamphlet, consists of those born between the mid-1960s and the mid-1970s – those late baby-boomers, he claims, 'who know how to wear smart casual, dress conservative, but just do not vote Conservative'. In the 2005 general election, Boys Smith points out, only 25 per cent of Generation Gap voted Conservative – 8 per cent less than the national average. Winning back Generation Gap, according to

46

Boys Smith, is the Tories' most important challenge. The party that can capture it, he predicts, will win the next election.

No one would deny the problem. The last in-depth study of the British Conservative party, back in 1992, found the average age of a Tory party member to be sixty-two. Since then, the party has ossified even further. But political parties only feel as young as the leaders they elect. Many New Labour favourites, after all, were elevated beyond their station in 1997 solely because they were young enough not to seem tarnished with the trauma of Labour's past. Cameron thinks he can work the same magic.

Generation Gap, according to Boys Smith, is just coming to political maturity, and beginning to inveigle its advance guard into a pivotal role in national life. Its members, he argues, are both economically and socially liberal, but less inclined to vote along economic lines. Who needs the laborious business of rustling up a political programme when you can rustle up a demographic group in need of a party? But both Boys Smith and his new leader have forgotten something. While oldies still vote in their droves, if only through force of habit, those paragons of social conscience in Generation Gap are much less likely to bother. Before he can persuade them of the merits of his shiny new Conservative party, Cameron needs to turn an army of disenchanted thirty-somethings not yet coloured by party affiliation back towards representative politics. He has his work cut out.

Good Business

British political parties may well be awash with donations from shady sources, but at least we now know that the money goes to a good home. The cash-strapped Conservative party, it was revealed in 2006, was forking out £23,000 a month for the services of one marketing guru and ally of David Cameron called Steve Hilton. A veteran of the 'Demon Eyes' attack on Tony Blair in 1997, Hilton subsequently changed tack to set up a branding consultancy advising big companies on how to be ethical. Now he is teaching the Conservative party how to be good, too.

Ethics is a healthy industry to be in. Thirty years ago, the economist Milton Friedman argued that the 'social responsibility of business is to maximize its profits'. While companies are still out to maximize their profits, they have recently begun to take on the added burden of relieving our conscience. One of the biggest growth industries in Britain and America is in programmes for corporate social responsibility. Starbucks associates its brand with support for 'fair trade' and eco-friendly coffee cups; Nokia wants to fight learning disabilities; Nike has even trumpeted itself as helping Native Americans combat diabetes. With traditional belief systems in steep decline, people are casting around for new affiliations and sources of wisdom. In the hands of the brand managers, our political vacuum looks like a gap in the market.

Hilton thinks that brands could go even further. 'Wouldn't it be good business for business to be good?' he wonders, at the beginning of his 2002 book *Good Business*. Plainly not, if it involved giving away all the profits, but Hilton has a sleeker alternative in mind. People may feel removed from politics, he argues, but brands are still capable of capturing their imagination. Hilton berates the anti-globalization activists for lacking a coherent alternative. Rather than complain about the malign influence of brands, he suggests, why not use them to reintroduce politicians to their electorate, and to engineer social change? Companies, for their part, might find that doing good works helps the brand stand out from the crowd and improves profitability.

But for all its can-do jauntiness, *Good Business* is a dull book, full of demonstrable falsehoods such as 'We are all capitalists now' and 'McDonald's is one of the most democratic institutions on the planet'. But if, as he suggests, corporations become our moral guardians, is there room left for real citizens? The result is to outsource political activism to corporations in return for the price of their products. It is only because of the weakness of politics that brands such as Nike are able to intervene to pick up the pieces of our ethical life. Now the Tories are in the humiliating position of following their lead.

Gotcha Politics

What do the spinners do after the age of spin? The answer, as the mainstream media caves in under pressure from huge armies of bloggers and amateur cameramen, is that things get all the more murky. Despite all those earnest lectures about the power of the web and new communication gizmos to reinvigorate democratic debate, their most telling contribution thus far has been to accentuate so-called 'gotcha politics' – the tendency of politics to descend into a hunt in which rival teams of campaign managers ferret out evidence of slip-ups, miscues and scandals involving their rivals. Now it is not only the professionals who are spinning, but just about everyone with access to a camera phone, or within typing distance of a muckraking blog.

Examples of this new kind of spin abound. What about the apparent drunkenness of President Nicolas Sarkozy at a press conference with President Vladimir Putin in June 2006, captured for posterity and somehow leaked to an appreciative audience on YouTube? Then there was the incident, late the previous year, when former Democratic presidential contender John Kerry was forced to issue a humiliating apology after he was taped telling college students that they'd better study hard or else they might 'get stuck in Iraq'. Even before that, the former Republican senator for Virginia, George Allen, had been caught in the act of calling someone a 'macaca', an apparently racist epithet for someone of Indian descent, in a video which has already been viewed on YouTube over half a million times.

The raison d'être of this highly partisan army of amateur spinners is to punch holes in the polished professionalism which has grown up around politicians. They see it as their job to poke, needle, manipulate or edit politicians until they appear to lose the plot or forget their prepared lines – and they have even fewer qualms about spreading rumour, disinformation and innuendo than professional spin-doctors. Whatever they tell you on the web, as a long-time teetotaller it is highly unlikely that Nicolas Sarkozy would be seen drunk at a press conference; George Allen's jibe was crass and reprehensible, but it was delivered to the camera of a hostile campaign worker who had been stalking him for some time; even John Kerry's botched joke – a quip about President Bush's foreign policy adventures – was carefully edited out of its context to make it look like a joke about American servicemen.

These are the stories which are being spun out of reach of the mainstream media in the wild west of the worldwide web, and those who work in political communications are being forced to pay attention. The date when party politics lost its innocence to the media is usually traced to 1960, when a fresh-faced John F. Kennedy triumphed over a shifty-looking Richard Nixon in a televised debate for the American presidency. Politics had entered the broadcast age, and politicians of all kinds responded by teaching themselves how to be professional performers for the camera. When hand-held video recorders first began to fly off the shelves at the end of the last decade, futurologists convinced themselves that it would usher in a new and more authentic era of people's media. Little did they know it would turn out like a political version of *Candid Camera*.

Confronted with the democracy of spin, professional spinners will be tempted to go into overdrive and script every moment of their candidate's lives. That would be the wrong move entirely. Jaded with polished professionalism, the politicians who want to thrive in this new media age need to watch what they say, but they also need to come across as rough and ready media amateurs who reveal something of the real person beneath. Think of George Bush, whose regular gaffes and verbal meanderings have only endeared him to the American electorate. Or of Gordon Brown, whose media image as an aloof fuddy-duddy may yet turn out to be an asset.

The kind of transparency demanded in the democracy of spin

will bring its own kind of tyranny. Amateur hour is upon us, and the only way to beat them is to join them.

Happiness

'Happiness, happiness,' the Liverpool comedian Ken Dodd likes to croon, 'the greatest gift that I possess. I thank the Lord that I've been blessed with more than my share of happiness.' The song was a hit record for Dodd back in the 1960s, and ever since then he has used it as a finale for his stage show.

Dodd's *joie de vivre* took a knock in the 1980s when he was accused of diddling the taxman, but more recently his philosophy of the good life has been triumphantly vindicated. 'Happiness' has become one of the most influential ideas of our time, and an army of thinkers – sociologists, psychologists, philosophers, neuroscientists, economists – have taken up their tickling sticks to distribute it. Hardly a week goes by without another study telling us what happiness is and how useful it can be. One recent survey by American psychologists, for example, discovered that happy people are generally more productive and more successful, and that 'happy nations' are likely to be more prosperous than miserable ones.

The notion of happiness is hardly new to the world of ideas, and everyone from the Ancient Greeks to the English utilitarian philosophers has found it useful. The reason why today's intellectuals have pounced on it, however, is that they suspect that we are not as happy as we should be. 'On average,' Richard Layard estimates in his influential book *Happiness: Lessons from a New Science* (2005), 'people are no happier today than people were fifty years ago.' But is there any reason why they should be? Happiness is the most willowy and ephemeral of emotions. Despite the best efforts of the neuroscientists, it is notoriously tricky to define and quantify. The new theorists of happiness believe themselves to be against materialism – buying more things, they claim, has failed to make us any happier – but it is the height of consumerist arrogance to assume that happiness is something that we can demand more of, as if it were tinned fruit or money in the bank. In the American Declaration of Independence in 1776, Thomas Jefferson wrote that all men are endowed with certain inalienable rights, and 'that among these are Life Liberty and the pursuit of Happiness'. To give us the means to pursue happiness is all well and good, but to promise to deliver it ready-made is a bridge too far. Worse, the happiness gurus are in danger of making our innermost emotions into the instruments of public policy rather than ends in themselves. If we could only be made happier, they reckon, we could be better workers and better citizens.

But the great thing about happiness, Aristotle believed, is that it cannot be a means to anything else – it is entirely useless, and prized for its sheer abandon. No longer: as being chipper is good for the economy and for the country, we can all look forward to the same fate as those service workers who are contractually obliged to smile.

Incentivization

How much money would it take for you to want to make a baby? President Vladimir Putin of Russia recently announced a cash prize – about £5,000 – for every Russian woman who does him the favour of having a second child. It was a typically bawdy display of Putin populism, as well as a desperate measure aimed at renewing Russia's shrivelling population. But in a country where the average income is a fraction of our own, it was also a generous incentive to get cracking.

Beyond the birth rate, governments everywhere are falling back on financial incentives to nudge us in the right direction. The British government's working families tax credit system, according to research published by the University of London in April 2006, has had the unintended consequence of giving rise to an extra 50,000 married couples over the past seven years – all of whose nuptials, researchers concluded, were precipitated by the cash they trousered when they went up the aisle.

But do such incentives work? The idea that anything can be solved with a simple cash bung or financial slap on the wrist is one whose roots lie in a school of economic analysis sometimes called 'public choice theory'. Dating from 1950s America, its starting point is that people – in politics and society, as well as in the market – are concerned only with getting more of what they already want. The best way to steer people towards the right decisions, these theorists assumed, was to offer 'selective incentives' – sweeteners only available if the correct action is taken.

Gradually, public choice theory began to expand its empire into analysing social institutions such as marriage, voting and the penal system. The idea was further popularized by the recent bestseller *Freakonomics* (2006), in which American economists Steven D. Levitt and Stephen J. Dubner implied that almost any social ill could be ameliorated by looking afresh at the incentives on offer to those who are involved in it. 'Incentives,' they announced triumphantly at the beginning of their book, 'are the cornerstone of modern life. And understanding them – or, often, ferreting them out – is the key to solving just about any riddle, from violent crime to sports cheating.'

But if selective incentives are the cornerstones of modern life, that is surely only because we have put them there. Having babies is an expensive business, for example, and any help is surely welcome, but the declining fertility rate in most Western countries can hardly be explained away by economic factors alone. As the politics of left and right have collapsed into one another, however, the technocratic solution of offering selective incentives to reward appropriate behaviour increasingly takes the place of a battle over what is right or wrong. The pro-marriage lobby, for example, can encourage us to get married for a tax break, and the anti-abortion lobby can try to pay women to forgo terminations.

But once we admit that a system of sweeteners and fines can rearrange us like iron filings in a school physics experiment, it's difficult to know where to draw the line. How about paying everyone a tenner to vote, or fining them a tenner when they don't? Tweaking the incentives on offer is surely a superficial approach to achieving lasting social change. The really freaky thing about doling out selective incentives, it turns out, is that in doing so governments are trying to reduce deeply held beliefs and important cultural values to the sordid matter of a bung.

Infomania

In the time I spent researching this short section, I have checked my email about fifty times, played with Google about twenty times, checked a newspaper search engine five times, taken three telephone calls and replied to a text from a friend who is on holiday abroad. I am, dear reader, suffering from an acute case of infomania.

Infomania is said to be a kind of attention deficit disorder for the communications age, where raw information is available more readily than running water. It is the condition of impaired concentration brought about by the constant distraction of 'always on' technology such as email and text-messaging. The idea was further popularized when an Institute of Psychiatry study in 2005 discovered that the excessive and neurotic use of communications technology was affecting the intelligence of British workers. More than half of the 1,100 respondents to the study confessed that they always responded to an email 'immediately' or as soon as possible; more than one in five admitted that they would interrupt a meeting to do so. Workers distracted by email and phone calls were judged by the surveyors to suffer a lack of concentration equivalent to the loss of a good night's sleep – more than twice that encountered among marijuana smokers.

Infomaniacs, it seems, are the kind of people who talk distractedly in conversation while thumbing text-messages about nothing much, or who interrupt a romantic dinner to check email on their BlackBerry. The fantasy of the infomaniac is that the information is important and they are its vital recipients – as likely as not, they will break off a conversation only to find that Pam from Accounts is having a leaving party, or that they can make their penis longer by wiring some money to a company based in Nevada. In any case, the condition of infomania is hardly good for productivity. When researchers at the University of California shadowed information workers in offices to find out what they got up to, they found that they got only three minutes' work done before being diverted – more often than not, by an email or a text-message.

The condition of infomania is easy to cure, however. It strikes only when we allow trivial information to enslave us rather than the other way around. Infomaniacs who want to kick the habit, after all, only need reach as far as the off button. While going through the painful process of information cold turkey, it may be therapeutic for them to have a conversation.

Yet the malady is not restricted merely to text-messaging and email. In the era of twenty-four-hour news bulletins, infomania is exacerbated by the deluge of news coverage puffed up with speculation and relentless trivia. Sharing some of the blame here are endless surveys, usually undertaken among sparse population samples and designed chiefly to create a media splash on behalf of their sponsors. The best contribution they could make to alleviating infomania, even the researchers at the University of California might have reflected, would be to consign their research results straight to the bottom drawer.

Libertarian Paternalism

Getting ahead as a modern politician is about mastering the art of compromise, and where better to start than with your ideas. Who anywhere on the political spectrum is now prepared to put the case for an unbridled libertarianism? On the other hand, very few of our politicians are prepared to argue for a nanny-style paternalistic relationship between government and its people.

So it was that many of our politicians began to converge on a concept known as libertarian paternalism. It started life in a 2003 paper by two of America's most innovative economists, Cass R. Sunstein and Richard H. Thaler, and its novelty was to move deftly beyond the stale dichotomy between state regulation and our freedom to consume as much as we like, accepting that we should all be free to choose, while the government nudges us in the right direction.

Libertarian paternalism takes its cue from the fact that people's preferences are ill-formed and often contradictory, the product of our disordered psyche. What is missing from the freedom we enjoy as consumers, argue its enthusiasts, is any means of ranking the different choices that we want to make. I love smoking, for example, but I also hate myself for it and aspire to a healthier, smoke-free lifestyle. A political philosophy that only registered my immediate desire for a cigarette would look stupid, as few of us are such slaves to desire that we can be said to be unaware of the consequences of our own actions. Likewise, a philosophy that stamped on my ability to choose would end up looking brutal and austere. What libertarian paternalism does is to step into the breach, with 'soft' policy tools for moral persuasion, such as public health initiatives – things designed to save us from ourselves, but without relieving us of the burden of making up our own minds. In our preferences we are creatures of habit and as government can never be entirely neutral, it is right for our elected representatives to second-guess our desires and point us in the direction of more 'informed' choices.

At the end of June 2006, the Tory leader David Cameron, doubtless nudged into action by his personal team of policy wonks, threw in his lot with libertarian paternalism. The new Conservative party, he argued, should steer a course between amoral indifference and coercive social engineering – one that operates, he claimed, 'by persuasion, not by power'. Daddy knows best, in other words, even though he refuses to tell you how to run your life. It was an astute piece of politicking, but Labour's policy wonks have, a little like Goldilocks, been there before him. Much of Labour's strategy for its third election term has been based on second-guessing our behaviour through 'soft' policy tools for moral persuasion. The recent government-funded 'Dad Pack' for new fathers, for example, was just such a wheeze – fun enough not to look preachy, but with a serious message.

Cameron thinks he can find some political traction in contrasting his libertarian paternalism with Gordon Brown's economic control-freakery, but Brown will doubtless soon declare himself a libertarian paternalist too. The battle of the dads has barely begun, and if Cameron wants a really fresh idea he had better go back to the family drawing board.

Life-Caching

Google's plan for world domination continues apace. But even while its Oompa-Loompas have been busy scanning the world's libraries for words and pictures to put into a digital archive, the worldwide web has steadily been filling up with something else. As portable hard-drive devices such as iPods become widespread and as it becomes easier to store stuff online, many of us have taken to archiving our lives in digital form, either as personal diaries or for sharing with others.

The phenomenon caught the attention of the Zeitgeist-surfers at Trendwatching.com in Amsterdam, who have dubbed it 'life-caching'. 'An almost biblical flood of "personal content",' they say, 'is being collected, and waiting to be stored to allow for ongoing trips down memory lane.' Life-caching is being driven by camera phones, online photo sites such as flickr.com and the increasingly generous storage allowances of email providers. Despite all the hype about blogging, much of the blogosphere, too, is clogged up with individuals' online diaries chattering about their everyday lives.

The desire to preserve our experiences is as old as the diary. But digitization and the internet have helped overturn our notions about privacy; we are now happy to share intimacies and personal details with people on the other side of the world that we would balk at telling our friends. They have given us the space, too, to funnel our life experiences into the electronic ether. Just as businesses are obsessed with squirrelling away all their records in an electronic archive, many of us are spending huge quantities of our time deep-freezing our lives into digital storage.

Life-caching is still a phenomenon in its infancy. As the gadgets become more ubiquitous and the storage space cheaper, media monoliths are vying with each other to get in on the action. Samsung's recent 'Show Your World' advertising campaign in America, for example, incites camera-phone owners to record their daily lives and turn them into movies. In one of the commercials, an actress films herself falling in love, hanging out at a hip club and at a fashion show. The tagline? 'The most vibrant way to capture and share life experiences with family and friends.'

But as more of our lives end up in a digital archive, the danger is that those archives become more real and more pressing than anything else. And think for a minute about the legacy that we want to bequeath future generations. Do we want our virtual memory bank on the worldwide web to consist of the sum of human knowledge transferred from our libraries, or our holiday slides writ large? Whatever else it does, life-caching will make it even more difficult to separate the wheat from the electronic chaff. We have become electronic hoarders, and the worldwide web is becoming less of a treasure trove than an electronic dumping ground.

The Long Tail

Those who are bored rigid by the selection in Blockbuster and their local multiplex might take comfort from the latest idea to create a buzz in media and technology circles. The 'long tail' is the idea developed by Chris Anderson on the pages of *Wired*, the magazine of which he is editor-in-chief, which has now appeared as a book of the same name. In the digital world, said Anderson, the way that media and entertainment businesses sell their products has been thrown into a tailspin that has not yet been fully appreciated. The long tail is made up of those millions of books, films and albums that sell only a trickle of copies every year – those whose presence on a company's sales chart form a line that tails off downwards. As everything migrates into digital bits and becomes less constrained by the demands of physical space, however, these lesser-selling products will increasingly come into their own.

The future of media and entertainment lies not in landing a few big fish, then, but in hooking the hundreds of thousands of minnows that together can be sold for much more. For every punter who strolls out of Waterstone's with a heavily plugged copy of the latest Lynne Truss, there is another who will not rest until they have tracked down an obscure volume on Venetian calligraphy, or the Bob Monkhouse bumper book of jokes. Add up all those niche and downright obscure purchases and you have a business worth billions. If the twentieth-century entertainment industry was about hits and blockbusters, according to Anderson, the twenty-first will be about a multiplicity of misses. The long tail, he predicts, is giving rise to an entirely new economic model for the media and entertainment industries, and one that is just beginning to show its mettle. Forget about plugging a few bland bestsellers and leaving all the good books to languish in the storeroom in single file, unplugged and unread. Half of Amazon's book sales, he points out, come from outside its top 130,000 titles.

As the long tail matures and people delve deeper into the digital archive, collecting recommendations as they go, they will find that their taste is not as dull as they had imagined. The long tail will become a huge jumble sale of everything that has ever existed, and most of us will be keen to rummage through it. For those online retailers and distributors who are blessed with a huge back catalogue, it will be wonderful news. It hardly solves the problem, though, of how to find and invest in new creative talent. In the long tail, the offbeat, quirky and the independent may find it easier to gain an audience, but the income they take home from the jumble sale will scarcely be enough to fund the bus fare home.

Maturialism

Get your motor runnin'. Head out on the highway. Lookin' for adventure. If you recognize Steppenwolf's lyrics, the chances are that you are middle-aged and long over the hill. But you are also likely to covet a swanky new Harley Davidson and the wind in your hair. And with the children having left home and the money behind you, there seems no reason why you can't go wild.

The average age of the owner of a Harley-Davidson motorbike, it is well known, has accelerated from thirty-eight to forty-six in the past decade. 'Born-again bikers' have become emblems of a spectacular inversion of social norms, and one that is whetting the appetite of marketeers and the media. Baby-boomers – the bulging demographic cohort born between 1946 and 1964 – present an enormous potential market for clever companies. Over the next ten years, the biggest growth in the population will be in those aged between thirty-five and sixty. Many of these will be at the peak of their earning potential; many more will have benefited from 'windfall' inheritances. The non-conformist baby-boomers, say the pundits, have revolutionized every stage of life through which they have passed – and now they look set to upturn the business of growing old. And because they refuse to relinquish the attributes of rebellious youth, the new middle-aged – unlike previous generations – continue to crave the attentions of marketeers and advertisers.

Maturialism is the idea – coined by the Zeitgeist-watchers at Trendwatching.com in Amsterdam – to describe this determination by baby-boomers to treat themselves to high-end goods, services and experiences simply because they can afford them. Some market sectors, it is obvious, can hardly fail to profit from the vanity and the materialism of ageing boomers. Pharmaceutical and cosmetics manufacturers stand to prosper as a result of their anxieties about their beauty, health and well-being. So excited are travel marketeers, too, that they have invented a new marketing segment – the 'bloomers', late-flowering baby-boomers who have the time and the funds to travel. Youth brands such as Wrigley's and Kellogg's, meanwhile, are busy repositioning their brands as accessories to the distinctive joys of mid-life. Ad agencies, keen to placate middle-aged women, are hiring so-called 'greybabes' such as Andie MacDowell, Julianne Moore and Jerry Hall. Age Concern and *Saga* magazine, those upholders of the older generation, are perennially giving themselves a youthful makeover. Manufacturers in most advanced industrial countries are taking to maturialism like ducks to water. For the past five years, fashion designers in Italy such as Prada, Gucci and Armani have been offering special lines aimed at the older customer – complete with looser fits, higher waist- and neck-lines and colours which accent pallid skin. In the United States, mega-publishers such as Penguin and HarperCollins recently announced their plans to produce bigger books, with larger print, to attract older customers who are having trouble reading. The new books will be half an inch taller than existing formats, and will be more expensive.

Yet the determination of older people to treat themselves to the best and live life to the full can have unforeseen consequences. As the number of 'born-again' middle-aged bikers has increased, so has the number of fatalities as they increasingly wrap their expensive Harley-Davidsons around lampposts. Sometimes baby-boomers really do want to die before they get old.

The Menaissance

'I am a man first and foremost,' Zinedine Zidane told French television in an effort to explain how his head managed to make contact with an Italian footballer's chest in the closing minutes of the 2006 World Cup final. Coupled with David Beckham's lame exit from the same tournament, the rise of anti-hero Zidane was immediately hailed as a departure in our attitudes to malehood. Preening, sarong-sporting metrosexuality was so over, the style gurus declared; long live the hard man.

Sure enough, something interesting has been going on. The same summer of 2006 saw the launch of *Superman Returns*, a knowing, post-September 11 gamble on whether we can still take the testosterone-powered superhero seriously. The latest genre in the books trade, according to the *New York Times*, is known as fratire – a booze-and-birds literary riposte to chicklit, with titles like *Real Men Don't Apologise, The Alphabet of Manliness* and *I Hope They Serve Beer in Hell.* When even that moustachioed icon of the 1970s, Burt Reynolds, is enjoying a revival, you know something is up.

In North America, where the resurrection of interest in traditional masculinity is gathering pace, cultural commentators suspect we might be on the brink of a 'menaissance' – an era in which we will learn once again to glorify 'real men'. A dollop of intellectual respectability has been added to the mix by a Harvard professor of government, Harvey C. Mansfield. In 2006, Professor Mansfield took a breather from writing tomes on representative government in order to publish a book entitled *Manliness*, in an attempt to reclaim traditional masculinity from what he considers to be quaintness and obsolescence.

Our attempts to create a gender-neutral society, according to Prof. Mansfield, have had the unfortunate effect of stripping men of their boldness; the values and pursuits we traditionally associated with masculinity are increasingly ridiculed or pathologized. Women, he argues, want real men, but they are just as confused about what they want them to be as men are confused about who they are. He believes that essential differences between the sexes should be accepted and celebrated. Manliness, he assures us, is rooted in values like stoicism, strength of character, assertiveness and decisiveness, the confidence to take risks and to be a gentleman whenever necessary. 'A manly male isn't sensitive,' says Mansfield. 'He doesn't care what you're thinking, but he'll be faithful.'

There is more than a whiff of pathos in Mansfield's elegy for the lost values of manliness, because the real world can only let him down. It is not as if most men, enraged by a diet of low-fat yoghurt and *Men's Health* magazine, have decided to take to the hills in an attempt to rediscover the masculine virtues. What passes for manhood in popular culture – the guy who cracks open a can of beer and puts his feet up – is less about what men do than what they eat, drink and wear. The burst of enthusiasm for manliness is an unabashed ploy by advertisers and market-eers to reacquaint themselves with their male audience; it is as cosmetic a phenomenon as those woman-friendly ads that portray men as Neanderthals who don't know how to fill a washing machine.

Like the latest *Superman* film, the new manliness is a pastiche of masculinity as much as anything else. Just as Clark Kent and Superman are one and the same, the metrosexual and his leery, backsliding alter ego are only two sides of the same tortured psyche. Don't tell Zinedine Zidane – he might take it badly – but the hellraisers of the menaissance probably still live with their mums.

Muscular Liberalism

In the middle of April 2006, a brand-new British political movement, the Euston Manifesto Group, charged forth from behind the foetid turrets of the blogosphere and into real life. Named after the area of London where the plotters got together for their inaugural meeting, the manifesto was born out of frustration among sections of the left with the anti-war movement.

Prominent bloggers, journalists, activists and academics have already lent it their support.

The Euston Manifesto Group is a tiny alliance – arguments about it still ricochet around the worldwide web – but one which is indicative of a broader shifting of intellectual chairs. To many, its signatories are known as 'muscular liberals' – to distinguish them, presumably, from the flabby and weak-willed ones. There is much that is useful and spirited about their manifesto: the signatories score some eloquent points against the left's opportunistic flirtation with radical Islam, its lazy anti-Americanism, and its retreat into flaccid relativism. Nor does it make any sense to label them as neoconservatives and apologists for American imperialism. The American neoconservative right and the British muscular liberals might have arrived at similar positions, but they did so from vastly different premises and backgrounds.

A better clue to the convictions of the muscular liberals can be found in the work of one its most thoughtful supporters, the American writer Paul Berman. In his partly autobiographical new book, *Power and the Idealists*, Berman, a former 1960s' radical and inhabitant of a Maoist commune, tracks the political trajectory taken by many of his peers on the international new left as they moved towards the political establishment – the former NATO Secretary-General Javier Solana, for example, and Sergio Vieira de Mello, the UN diplomat killed by a suicide bomber in Baghdad in 2003. The generation of sixties' political radicals known as the soixante-huitards, he argues, were the orphans of a Europe that had capitulated to Fascism and Nazism. For many of the European radicals, their politics were a rebellion against this past; they were haunted by their parents' failures and wanted to be sure they would resist when the time came.

The best of them, Berman says, felt their way towards political responsibility in the 1990s by standing up to Serbian expansionism in the Balkans. He reserves his bitterest ire for former leftists such as Daniel Cohn-Bendit and Joschka Fischer, who threw in their lot with NATO military intervention in Bosnia and Kosovo but drew the line at the invasion of Iraq. The true legacy of 1960s idealism has evolved into anti-totalitarian progressive politics that will have no truck with dictatorships or large-scale abuses of human rights.

Berman's is an intriguing and nuanced argument, but it would be just as easy to turn it on its head. Amid the fevered rhetoric of 1968, the student left lobbed the labels of Fascism and Nazism indiscriminately, and tended to the conclusion that there was little difference between the post-war democracies and totalitarian regimes. When they try to enforce their demands for global democracy and human rights decades later, the most vulgar of the muscular liberals make rallying cries out of 'Serbo-fascism' or 'Islamo-fascism', and are tempted to exaggerate human rights abuses into genocide and authoritarianism into Fascism. Like an intellectual dads' army, they are hunting around for Nazis when there are none to be found. The radical students were young as well as idealistic, and had more excuse.

Neurotheology

In 2005, in Britain's first televised exorcism, a man known only as Colin was hooked up to start-of-the-art brain-imaging equipment in east London and prayed over by a po-faced Anglican priest. The programme provoked some predictable anger from the moral majority at the time, but the defence of its commissioning editors was more novel. The exorcism, they said, was not a reality TV thriller but a serious-minded scientific experiment into what happens to the brain during possession by evil spirits. It was, they claimed, field research in a new discipline called neurotheology.

Neurotheology is the scientific study of what happens to brain activity during religious or spiritual experiences and an attempt to divine a neural basis for human spirituality. The word itself dates from Aldous Huxley's utopian 1962 novel *Island*, but the science is a more recent development, made possible by advances in brain-imaging. The idea is to use the latest tools available within the disciplines of psychology and neuroscience to detect which parts of the brain are active during spiritual experiences. Scientists have long been puzzled, for example, by the fact that some sufferers from epilepsy appear to experience religious hallucinations or revelations during their seizures. Neurotheology, its supporters claim, might tell us why.

By tracing the neural origins of religious experiences, the more radical advocates of neurotheology hope to understand not only how brain activity mirrors spiritual experiences but also how it can cause those experiences. The discipline first entered public consciousness in the late 1980s, when Michael Persinger, an Ontario neuroscientist, used a helmet filled with magnets to surround the skulls of his subjects, stimulating their temporal lobes with a weak magnetic field. The result, according to Persinger, was to induce a 'mystical experience' in four out of five people taking part. Religious epiphanies, he concluded, were simply bursts of electrical activity in the frontal lobes which could be triggered by a variety of emotions or physical stimuli.

If we take neurotheology literally, the implications are severe. If God lies within our brains rather than within our souls, it seems likely that we invented God rather than the other way around. Some neurologists go further, arguing that religion is a mere figment of delusional mental processes, a kind of mental illness. On the other hand, if one part of the brain is 'wired' to have religious experiences, it might explain why religion refuses to die in the modern world. Given that the soul can be a fickle instrument, if God has reserved Himself a place within our brains it may simply be His insurance policy against atheism.

But it is not just the religious who balk at some of the implications of neurotheology. It rather devalues any kind of human spirituality if the same effect can be conjured up with the help of a few magnets. The mysteries involved in the human subconscious might well be tracked to blips in our brain activity, but it remains doubtful that it can be explained by them.

The New Puritans

The first rule for following social trends is to throw out *Vogue* and *GQ* and take out some subscriptions to trade magazines. According to a survey conducted by those style mavens on *The Grocer* magazine, the demand for home breadmakers is rising faster than a loaf in a hot oven – from sales of 33,700 in 1997 to 445,000 in 2001 alone, a more than tenfold increase in just four years. What the rise of the great British breadmaker signifies is the premium which many of us have begun to place on natural-ness, on knowing how food products are made and the sources of ingredients. Authenticity is the new luxury, and buying a home breadmaker is the first rung on the ladder to acceptability among the faithful.

At least among marketeers and advertisers, these modern seekers after authenticity have become known as the new purit-ans. They are those well-to-do professionals who invest time and money in researching the provenance and pedigree of what they consume. However, a taste for organic food is a necessary but not a sufficient condition for the badge of new puritan. What is crucial to them is not only how a product is produced but where, and with what raw materials. There is a good deal of snob value, for example, in knowing not only that the wine they buy hails from a particular region of France but also from a particular estate in the area. For the new puritans, sourcing one's produce has become an instrument of social competition, and one which is becoming more exacting all the time – a superior olive oil, for example, might not just be traced to Italy, but to a particular estate in one of the nicer regions of Tuscany. Bottled water, whose label denotes its origins as French, is not enough: the new puritan needs to know exactly which mountain spring that bottled water came from – so that they can tell you while they pour it for you.

The new puritans would prefer to live in the country. But since to do so would be financially impractical and socially ruinous, they make do as best they can. Not content with having redeemed themselves, they are now advancing to take control of whole communities. Late in 2003, for example, a minor revolt began percolating through the drawing rooms of Parisian society. In an orchestrated series of attacks in the popular press, citizens and community representatives banded together to bemoan what they took to be the gravest threat to the health of their city: the city's new metropolitan elite and its quest for a blissfully quiet life. The arrival of the new 'quiétards' into an urban area was invariably accompanied by campaigns for traffic restrictions, noise control and speed limits, making it harder for shops to receive deliveries and people to travel. The metamorphosis of the new puritans into a social movement – dedicated to a pared-down approach to modern life, free from both artifice and interruption – is certainly not limited to France. In Italy, the success of the 'slow food' movement gave rise to one in favour of 'slow cities', dedicated to slowing the expansion of Starbucks and McDonald's, to reducing noise and to pedestrianizing whole areas. Since its origins with the Rome manifesto five years ago, thirty-three Italian cities have signed up to the League for Slow Cities and another sixteen are still awaiting approval. The movement's top brass are now considering applications from budding 'slow cities' in Brazil, Greece and Switzerland.

Good luck to them. But the problem with the new puritans is

that there is very little that is pure or authentic about baking your own bread in a consumer gadget, and very little quality in a life whose highest priority is a bit of peace and quiet. The home breadmaker is simply determined not to put his trust in his local baker, and instead resorts to doing all the work and the research himself. For the new puritans, the twentieth century happened almost entirely in vain.

The New Utopianism

For some years now, the hottest thing on the international left circuit has been President of Venezuela Hugo Chávez. No matter that he is a former army officer with populist tendencies; on his regular world tours, Chávez draws appreciative and mildly nostalgic crowds wherever he goes. For many, Chávez's celebrity is evidence of a revival of the utopian impulse. In the magazine *Foreign Affairs*, for example, the former Mexican Foreign Minister Jorge Castaneda recently linked Latin America's recent lurch leftwards to a new kind of utopianism, even if he concluded that Chávez himself was more of a populist than a utopian.

All this is a little unexpected. Just a few years ago, the modern idea of utopia – 500 years old, dating from the publication of Thomas More's *Utopia* in 1516 – had been banished to the periphery of political theory. Now it has acquired a new respectability. In their latest books, two of America's leading left intellectuals, Fredric Jameson and Russell Jacoby, make it their mission to reinvigorate utopia for a contemporary audience. Even the left-leaning British thinker David Marquand, disenchanted with New Labour's pragmatism, has recently argued that the left needs a utopian vision to see it through the twenty-first century.

Jacoby's book, *Picture Imperfect* (2005), is as good an example as any of the new breed. He points out that the idea of utopia is too readily thrown around as a term of abuse. Utopian has come to mean, he says, not just someone who has a difficult-to-swallow vision of a future society but anyone who is prone to violence in pursuit of their political ambitions. The Nazis are now regularly labelled as utopian, for example; likewise the men who flew planes into the World Trade Centre. Nor do utopias necessarily morph into dystopian purgatories, as Aldous Huxley implied that they must in *Brave New World* (1932). His wrath is reserved for the liberal thinkers of the post-war period – Hannah Arendt, Isaiah Berlin and Karl Popper – who flirted with radicalism in their youth but went on to build intellectual careers championing 'anti-utopianism', thus blackening its name for an entire generation.

Jacoby acknowledges the weaknesses of much of utopian thought. The problem with many visions of utopia is that they micromanage their blueprint of the future – laying down the law on interior furniture, for example, or what time dinner will be served in the commune. The world conjured up by William Morris in his 1890 book *News from Nowhere*, for example, looks worthy and uninviting – not somewhere many would want to be. Jacoby, however, claims to have unearthed a different tradition of utopian thinking that allows visions of the future to emerge more naturally from everyday reflections on music, poetry and literature. This kind of thinking, he says, can help open the window on stale political debate and let in the breeze.

Thoughts of utopia tend to prosper when progressive politics is powerless and lacks organization. But they are also useful as a weapon against the narrowing of the political imagination, as a kick against the current of pragmatism. Without them we are doomed to live in the present, with only technocrats for politicians and gadgets for visions. 'Our most important task at the present moment,' wrote Lewis Mumford in 1922, 'is to build castles in the air.' Try raising that the next time you're doorstepped by an election campaigner.

The Paradox of Choice

A couple of years ago, a skinny American political theorist called Barry Schwartz strolled into the Gap in search of a new pair of jeans. It took more time than he had bargained for. Schwartz had committed the cardinal error of entering into dialogue with a salesperson, and was in turn bombarded with a bewildering array of choices – slim fit, easy fit, relaxed fit, baggy, extra baggy. The selection was endless and, at least for a bookish social scientist such as Schwartz, more than a little daunting. But he tried them all on, just in case.

Schwartz emerged from his afternoon in the Gap with a pair of 'easy-fit' jeans and a grudge against the easy pervasiveness of choice in contemporary societies. 'Before these options were available,' he tells us on the second page of his cultishly influential book *The Paradox of Choice: Why More is Less* (2005), 'a buyer like myself had to settle for an imperfect fit, but at least purchasing jeans was a five-minute affair. Now it was a complex decision in which I was forced to invest time, energy, and no small amount of self-doubt, anxiety and dread.'

Schwartz's argument strikes at the heart of the 'hard' social sciences. It aims its daggers at the foundation stone of the disciplines of modern economics and political science – the idea of the 'utility-maximizing consumer'. The concept of such a consumer, whose desires are not specified other than to say that whatever he wants he wants more of it, bubbled up into the rest of the social sciences from neo-classical economics at about the same time as the economy of mass consumption emerged in the years after the Second World War. What is distinctive about Schwartz's argument is that he seeks to undermine from within the whole idea of the self-interested, utility-maximizing consumer. Using some of the most celebrated research on the theory of choice in the past thirty years, Schwartz argues that it ignores the fact that the very act of maximizing our desires tends to leave us all worse off. It assumes, for example, that it is rational to want more of a substance rather than just enough, that we are capable of making rational choices and of taking responsibility for those choices without regretting them later. Worst of all, it assumes that we make choices as isolated individuals.

Schwartz is right to argue that we face an abundance of choices, but his fashionable argument misunderstands the way the intellectual wind blows. What distinguishes contemporary society is less our lust for consumption than the diffidence and lack of morale with which we roll up to make those choices. If the intellectuals are on to anything, it is that the idea of ourselves as utility-maximizing consumers is not as healthy as it's cracked up to be – that it has foundered on our fatigue, the complexity of the decision-making process and our befuddlement when asked to assess risks. Far from being confident consumers, our decision-making as consumers is just as often fraught, guilt-ridden, inept or plain wrong-headed. The idea of the utility-maximizing consumer has its uses, but it turns out to be too shallow a foundation on which to construct either a social theory or a human identity. No sooner had the ideology of consumer choice won the intellectual battle against its statist competitors, it seems, than the cracks began to appear in its intellectual offering. It is as if – left to do its own thing – the whole idea of rational consumer choice over-vaulted itself and fell into a mire of complexity and incoherence.

Peer-to-Peer Surveillance

Ever left a garbled message on someone's answering machine because your phone went off by mistake, or listened to your own answering machine only to find the muffled conversation of a friend chattering away to someone else? In the age of ubiquitous digital equipment, with more cameras and mics lying around than there are on the set of *The Truman Show*, it is all too easy, unwittingly, to find our activities captured in digital form. We all know by now that we can be clocked on CCTV cameras, and snapped by camera phones, but it's only relatively recently that we have realized the vulnerability of a simple conversation. In September 2006, a speech by George Bush to mark the anniversary of Hurricane Katrina was interrupted by snatches of ladies' room gossip by a CNN News anchor who didn't realize her microphone was still switched on. A month before that, a private chat between Tony Blair and George was broadcast to the world via an unintentionally open mic, and two of the most powerful men in the world were caught joshing each other like superannuated rappers.

All of this can be filed under 'peer-to-peer surveillance' – the emerging idea that the constant operation of a whole range of digital devices will increasingly be used as evidence against us by parties other than the state. Thus far, much of the eavesdropping has been by accident, but there are more sinister opportunities to be exploited. Many of the new mobile phones come armed with the facility to record conversations, and digital voice-recorders are now so small as to be inconspicuous. As applications are designed to imprint the date, time and location in which photographs, conversations and videos are made, and mobile tracking devices increasingly allow us to pinpoint the location of others, we can predict consequences for everyday life as well as the legal system. If mobile phones are currently an accessory to infidelity, for example, a suspicious spouse may easily chance upon video, picture or location-based proof that you were not where you said you were, or commission evidence in support of their case. The notion of 'your word against mine' might soon be redundant; it will be 'your word against my digitally enhanced sound recording'.

Even so, there may be practical advantages to the spread of surveillance. Ever since Rodney King was videoed being beaten to a pulp by the Los Angeles police, trendspotters have waxed lyrical about the potential for digital evidence to hold wrongdoers to account. Thirty years ago, in the paranoid thriller *The Conversation*, Gene Hackman's professional wire-tapper becomes obsessed with the content of a conversation that he has been hired to listen in on, but subsequently finds that someone is bugging him too. At the time it was made, the film was supposed to be an indictment of the web of surveillance monitored by shady state functionaries in the military-industrial complex. But what if the surveilled and the surveillant turn out to be friends or colleagues? As reserves of trust in contemporary society continue to erode, we might begin to suspect that the other guy is wearing a wire.

Pension Fund Capitalism

People tend to think that the politics of pensions is yawningly dull: petty squabbles over a dwindling pot of savings and how to distribute it. So it is, at least when it comes to arguing about how much we ought to spend on pensions and when we should be entitled to them. The important point, though, is not how pensions are distributed but how they are accumulated.

Peter Drucker, one of the foremost business theorists of the twentieth century, who died in 2005, understood the pensions dilemma. He predicted, a full thirty years ago, that Western capitalism was moving towards what he called 'pension fund socialism', a kind of economy owned by the workers through the pension funds being reinvested in the economy on their behalf. Back in the 1970s, Drucker thought the money pensions could raise for investment might reignite a golden age of economic growth. As America was ahead of the game in pushing its pensions on to the money markets, he argued, it could claim to be the first truly socialist country in the world.

Since then, our economy has become much more reliant on pensions to keep it moving. But there is something odd about the way institutional investors are investing those pensions on our behalf. In his book *Pension Fund Capitalism* (2000), Professor Gordon Clark of Oxford University argues that understanding how pension funds spend their money is crucial to getting a handle on what is happening to the economy in which we work. Clark finds these pension funds and their agents guilty of something called 'loss aversion': being a little over-cautious, more worried about losing money than excited about making it. Some years ago, when Gordon Brown asked the investment banker Paul Myners to investigate what institutional investors do with our cash, he found evidence of herding and short-termism, and concluded 'savers' money is too often being invested in ways that do not maximize their interests'.

But what are those interests? Those of us who have invested our savings in pensions cannot afford to take chances. Unlike entrepreneurs, we will always prefer security because we need to know for certain how much money we can look forward to receiving on retirement. The result, many are beginning to suspect, is a contemporary economy that grows at a snail's pace and is hostile to the kind of risky investments in technology needed to bring our economy into the twenty-first century. In a perverse twist to the idea of a consumer economy, it turns out that most of our consumption is taken up with buying pensions and insurance. And since those investments are blunted by caution, it ensures that we remain tied to dull jobs in a service economy. Sometimes economics has as many twists and turns as a good novel.

Philoanthrocapitalism

The end of November 2006 saw the arrival on British television of yet another twist to the reality TV format. This new programme was called *The Secret Millionaire*, and it invited budding philanthropists to go undercover in impoverished urban communities in search of people whose lives they might turn around using their personal wealth. At the end of each episode, the secret Santas revealed themselves – surprise, surprise – and divvied out the cash to the most deserving among the poor.

The Secret Millionaire was unutterably bad television, but it mirrored an important shift within our culture. Among the very rich, giving away money has become even more fashionable than making it. Philanthropy's new practitioners tend, like their exemplar Bill Gates, to have made their own money rather than having inherited it. According to Charles Handy in his recent book *The New Philanthropists* (2006), they are 'hands-on, pioneering, and entrepreneurial' – and no longer prepared to give quietly and at arm's length. This phenomenon was first noticed in America, but is now beginning to become established over here. Whereas in 1989 three quarters of giving in Britain came from inherited wealth and only one quarter from self-made wealth, according to one recent index, the position is now reversed, with a full three quarters coming from self-made men and women. These new philanthropists take a more market-conscious approach to allocating their cash; they tend to come armed with spreadsheets and Powerpoint presentations and take a more active role in selecting and building their charitable ventures – and they want more bang for their charitable buck. A mini-industry of management consultants and intermediary agencies has now grown up to put rich people in touch with deserving causes – there is even talk of inaugurating a social stock market to match charitable merit with money.

Since there are so many things that modern government can't or won't do, there are plenty of causes which could benefit from the attention of the new philanthropists. No doubt, too, that some existing charities still spend too much of their money on administration costs, and that a gust of market discipline might breathe a little dynamism into the whole sector.

But there are dangers, too. Despite the best efforts of Channel 4, much of the new philanthropy packs little redistributive punch. The new philanthropists enjoy splashing their cash, but too often their largesse only comes free to those who can afford it – they like to endow glitzy arts organizations in their own name, for example, or scholarships at their educational alma mater. According to a recent article by Rob Reich, a political scientist at Stanford University, American philanthropy has done nothing to alleviate inequality. 'We should stop kidding ourselves', he concludes, 'that charity and philanthropy do much to help the poor.'

The new philanthropists want to make a difference, but without an understanding of the bigger picture, their efforts often look whimsical and arbitrary, and freighted with their often eccentric political or religious beliefs. They could benefit from realizing that, alongside commerce and government, they are minnows in a very big pond. At a time of increased sensitivity about donations from wealthy individuals to our political parties, it would be an irony if the super-rich were given a free hand to influence politics and our culture by the back door.

Playtime

Anyone remember Bagpuss? Bagpuss, for the uninitiated, was a lackadaisical toy cat who slept in the window of an antiques shop. Only after the shop closed did Bagpuss shake himself into life, whereupon our furry friend began making merry in the company of a platoon of mice and a wooden bird named Professor Yaffle.

If Bagpuss still has a pulse, he must be smoking fat cigars and toasting his good fortune to have lived in an era where it is possible to recycle pop-cultural artefacts from our youth. For, twenty years after his spot on British children's television was cruelly taken away, Bagpuss is making a comeback as a licensed brand; in its first three years, the Bagpuss franchise has churned out over a hundred different product lines, all of which are aimed at adults with fond memories of the lovable moggy. In the United States, the cultural equivalent of Bagpuss is a little toy car called Hot Wheels. When Mattel realized a couple of years back that it could exploit burgeoning nostalgia among the 40 million adults who grew up playing with Hot Wheels, the toy giant set about courting adult enthusiasts. Very soon the trickle of Hot Wheels spin-offs aimed at adults had become a flood.

All this is mere retail fluff, but it does point up one of the most cloying influential ideas of the twenty-first century – that it's good for adults to play. Nostalgia for yesterday's inanimate companions is only its most easily recognizable epiphenomenon. Did you know that in California there exists a business consultant called 'Dr Play' who, using props purchased from toyshops, helps chief executives rediscover their creativity in return for $3,000 a session? Or that a new division of the Danish toy company Lego has been set up to host two-day corporate strategy seminars in Lego Serious Play, a patented technique in which executives use specially made Lego blocks to help construct new business strategies? The aim, according to the sales pitch of the consultancy behind it, is to 'turn boardrooms into constructive playgrounds'. Despite the fact that the cost of a two-day workshop with trained Lego professionals costs in the region of $20,000, more than fifty major European companies have hired Lego's consultants, and many more in Canada and the US. Some companies have gone as far as to set aside special Lego rooms. INSEAD, the internationally respected graduate business school in France, is running courses using it.

So how did an idea which existed on the wilder fringes of social theory for the previous two centuries find its way into the mainstream? The resurrection of adult play, it turns out, coincided with a period in which the traditional building blocks of modern life – affiliation to career, trade union, religious belief and political party – slowly dissolved, and gave way to a gnawing uncertainty about life, the universe and everything. There is good reason, however, to be suspicious of the prophets of play power. More often than not, the ritual of adult play has none of the spontaneity and abandon of a child in the playground. Rather, it seems to function as an antidote to something else. For the babyboomers, an enthusiasm for play masks a stubborn fear of the process of growing old. Among young single professionals, it conceals an anxiety about settling down. Our love affair with toys represents a retreat from the adult world and an urge to wrap ourselves in the cotton wool of nostalgia. In the office, the idea of play acts as compensation for the lack of meaning within our working lives. For managers, it deflects attention from the real

Big Ideas PLAYTIME

problem of how to think up innovative new products and inspire their workforces.

Brian Sutton-Smith, world-leading play guru and former educationalist who was Dean of Play Studies at the University of Pennsylvania for seventeen years, argues that 'the opposite of play isn't work. It's depression. To play is to act out and be wilful, exultant and committed, as if one is assured of one's prospects.' His argument is revealing. When play offers a kind of reassurance – undertaken 'as if' one was certain of oneself and one's future – it begins to assume tragic proportions. Maybe the player is not such a fun guy after all. Maybe he is a man on the brink, bravely putting on a show.

Positive Liberty

Back in October 1997, as the political philosopher Isaiah Berlin lay on his deathbed in Oxford, he received a short note from Britain's new prime minister. What had intrigued Tony Blair was Berlin's celebrated distinction between two kinds of liberty: the simple 'negative' liberty of the individual to be free from external inter-ference or coercion, and the 'positive' liberty to take control of one's life and to play an active role in one's community.

Berlin's work on liberty was written at the height of the Cold War and was meant to encourage greater intellectual honesty among the communist left, some of whom were tempted to justify restrictions on negative liberty in the countries of the Soviet bloc by claiming to speak on behalf of a higher kind of freedom. But, like a precocious undergraduate with a bright idea, Blair wanted to quarrel with Berlin's injunction. Wasn't it true, he argued, that the value of negative liberty was pretty limited, and wasn't it right, then, to look for a new model of society that went beyond it? Either too ill or too bored, Berlin never got around to granting him a reply.

In retrospect, Tony Blair's letter to Isaiah Berlin in 1997 was hugely significant. New Labour and social democrats everywhere needed to talk about positive liberty, because after the end of the Cold War and the humbling demise of state socialism they needed to find a compelling reason to justify the actions of governments. Besides, the Tories had traditionally made it their business to champion the negative freedom of citizens to be left alone. It is hardly surprising, then, that a decade after Berlin's letter to Blair, New Labour is still getting its knickers in a twist over liberty. Delivering a lecture in December 2005, for example, Gordon Brown lauded the ideal of positive liberty and railed against 'the narrow view' of negative liberty as impoverished and backward. His New Deal embodied 'a positive view of liberty for all, the freedom to work'.

What are we to make of all this? Negative liberty, at least as conceived by everyone from Thomas Hobbes to Isaiah Berlin, serves to protect a minimum area of personal freedom from government – a private sphere beyond which the state should not trespass. Gordon Brown is asking us to think beyond the idea of negative liberty, to think about how a community can give its members the freedom to work. But was that really what Berlin had in mind when he talked about the positive freedom to play an active role in governing our lives and that of a community? Berlin's pessimistic assumption was that there must be a trade-off between positive and negative liberty, that to achieve more of the former you needed to throw off some of the latter. Gordon Brown is following suit, asking the long-term unemployed to forgo some of their negative liberty ('freedom from') precisely in order to win more positive freedom ('freedom to') for themselves and their communities. But Berlin was warning us against grand projects of social engineering which might end up curtailing our liberty along the way, not offering an intellectual justification for Jobclub. When Brown marshals positive liberty to support his authoritarian New Deal, he reminds us of precisely the kind of intellectual quackery that Berlin warned against.

The Precautionary Principle

What do the BSE crisis, the regular panics about paedophiles which haunt Western societies and the war in Iraq have in common? Only this – that in each case something called the 'precautionary principle' was wheeled out by governments as a justification for taking action on our behalf. The precautionary principle – the notion, put bluntly, that society is better off safe than sorry – is the most influential social policy idea of the last decade, and a breathless testament to the contagious power of ideas.

Until the early 1990s, the precautionary principle was the monopoly of environmentalists whose only concern was to find ways to help nip environmental pollution in the bud. But in a series of curious ideological shifts in the first half of the 1990s, it began to extend its domain into other areas of social policy such as food and child safety. The last decade of the twentieth century saw the precautionary principle become a new organizing staple for Western governments, who slowly changed their fundamental purpose from providing good things for their citizens to preventing bad things happening.

But how does it work? Most decisions that we take rely on a simple game of chance, in which we weigh the risks of doing nothing against the risks of applying greater political and military pressure. But rather than arriving at a decision by weighing the risks against the likelihood of their occurrence, the precautionary principle ranks alternative courses of action by their worst possible outcome in order to arrive at a decision. In terms of foreign policy, this means that if we are not sure about the arsenal and intentions of rogue states and there is a danger of a nuclear catastrophe, we are perfectly justified in having recourse to military preventive action. Donald Rumsfeld's ominous declaration in 2002 about the 'unknown unknowns' in dealing with the Iraqi nuclear threat, for example, is not as risible as his critics made out, but is hugely and silently indebted to the concept of the precautionary principle. Likewise, Tony Blair's post facto admission that he was right to wage war on Iraq given the information available to him at the time is perfectly consistent with his application of the precautionary principle.

The moral of the story, at least for anti-war environmentalists, is to handle principles with care. Without proper training – and a little like weapons of mass destruction – they are likely to blow up in your face.

Pre-heritance

Premature inheritance, just like premature ejaculation, can be a delicate and embarrassing subject to discuss. But it is increasingly common, and likely to cost us taxpayers very dearly in years to come.

Pre-heritance is the latest insurance industry jargon for the gifts that parents are increasingly doling out while they are still alive, in lieu of an inheritance on their death. More than four-fifths of Brits over fifty-five, according to a survey by the number crunchers at Datamonitor, would prefer to give to their children or grandchildren before they die. Nearly half said that they would consider releasing equity from their homes in order to do so.

All this, of course, might be no more than an attempt to dodge inheritance tax, which is stealthily widening its clutches to encompass more families every year. But it is also an acknowledgement that marching into adulthood has become a costly business. Degree courses and weddings, essential if you want to keep up with your peers, are getting more and more expensive. And then there is the pressure to give your little darlings a first heave on to the precarious housing ladder. More than half of home-owning parents of eighteen-to-twenty-nine-year-olds, according to a recent MORI poll, said they didn't think that their children would become homeowners without their support. The parents surveyed expected to bung their offspring up to £24,000 to help out.

Giving away a stream of handouts while still alive rather than a lump sum after death sounds like an entirely noble activity. It is surely more worthy than becoming a SKIER – the marketing acronym for the growing number of parents who would prefer to

Spend the Kids Inheritance on bungee-jumping lessons and expensive holidays. Then again, it might be part of the same basic phenomenon. Today's middle-aged and elderly are more enthusiastic than previous generations to splurge their cash, and less keen to defer gratification of their immediate desires. At the same time, surrounded by the detritus of a lifetime's accumulation of goods, they are rapidly losing interest in material possessions and are striving to acquire interesting experiences instead; witness everything from the growth in middle-aged adventure holidays to the boom in adult education.

But how does all this help explain the shift in favour of pre-heritance gifts? Instead of presenting you with a windfall when they die, a growing band of today's middle-aged and elderly would prefer to blow their capital on shared goods and shared experiences with you so that they can enjoy your reaction at the time. A good example is the growth of intergenerational travel, as parents treat children to expensive bonding holidays. That all-expenses-paid safari to Kenya with mother and father in tow? Just grin and bear it – and try to forget it's coming out of your inheritance.

Proletarian Drift

Who would have imagined that sleek stretch limos could hurtle their way so quickly through the class system? Not very long ago they were associated with the outrageously well heeled. Now they are chiefly populated by gaggles of girls on hen nights, tanked up on cheap wine and greeting passers-by with lewd hand gestures.

Stretch limos are an object lesson in the dangers of 'proletarian drift'.

Proletarian drift is a term favoured by marketeers and ad men, and describes the vulgarization of once luxurious products and services as they slowly trickle their way down to the lower orders. The term was first coined – and promptly abbreviated to 'prole drift' – by Paul Fussell, the curmudgeonly American cultural critic, in his 1983 book *Class: A Guide Through the American Status System*. A master of dyspeptic hauteur, Fussell railed against the tendency for any product or innovation to become tainted as soon as it began its descent into the grubby hands of the masses. Somewhat ahead of his time, Fussell argued that the education system was a perfect example of proletarian drift. A generation ago, he pointed out, it was only the rich or the very bright who went to university. With the steady expansion of higher education, however, it shed most of its exclusivity and its cachet.

The idea of proletarian drift has moved on since Fussell left it. Among fashion designers who want to retain the cachet of exclusivity, proletarian drift can now be a commercial liability. Much to the chagrin of haute couture, some of the most famous designer brands have quickly been colonized by the lower classes. Burberry, once the preserve of country-estate dwellers, is fast becoming the sine qua non of chav chic. At its most nuanced, prole drift is as much about taste as it is about produce. Buffets, for example, were once the preserve of ritzy hotels and the enormously affluent. Nowadays, however, every half-built holiday resort hotel has its own buffet, and guests who arrive in the dining room are confronted with bowls of lank salad and greying potatoes. Hotels at the higher end of the market have, as a consequence, turned against them.

At its most poisonous and patrician, on the other hand, prole drift becomes an all-encompassing reference to everything that has become lowbrow or infra dig. But not everything that has drifted as far as the proles can reliably be scorned. After all, everything from the foreign package holiday to the washing machine started out as a luxury before it became democratically available. Proletarian drift is really a kind of status anxiety, felt most viscerally by those who know that their money is no longer enough to separate themselves from the crowd. Forced to muck in with the oiks in economy class, all one can do is to turn up one's nose.

Protirement

If all work and no play makes for dull boys and girls, in the past couple of years we seem to have been leading more interesting lives. The backlash against the aspirational, go-getting yuppie of the 1980s began with the idea of 'downshifting' – relaxing one's commitment to career in favour of a better quality of life. Now, the notion of 'protirement' tries to take our revolt against the work ethic a step further. Whereas the downshifter clings to the world of work by going part-time, the protirer wants to leave the world of wage labour altogether and replace it with something more fulfilling.

Like most of these clumsy demographic categories, the idea of protirement began life in America. The word was first coined back in 1991 by Frederic M. Hudson, a self-help author and founder of a work-balance institute, as part of his effort to make retirement sound a little more fun. Recently, however, it has been used to describe a younger generation. In essence, the idea aims to put a more positive and more militant spin on the idea of dropping-out than downshifting. Whereas the downshifter spent impecunious afternoons watching daytime television and smoking Lambert & Butlers, the protirer is likely to be pursuing his own hobbies and ploughing his own furrow. And whereas the downshifter wanted only to change gear, the protiree wants to get a new car – or preferably a bicycle, given the austerity of the regime that he has imposed on himself.

A recent survey discovered that nearly half of all eighteen-to-thirty-five year olds in Britain were making plans to protire after the age of thirty, and that one in fifteen workers under thirty-five have made the break and walked out of their jobs. But where do they go? Men, it seems, aspire to a spot of organic farming, while the women favour a dose of charity work. Other protirers get creative – and spend their days twisting coat-hangers into objets d'art for sale on their market stall. Some of the most charming become florists, and find themselves wrapping up expensive flowers for the yuppies who can still afford them.

For the protirers, executive burnout arrives early, enabling them to short-circuit the whole idea of a career before they have had the misfortune to lift a finger. Faced with the prospect of working themselves into a frenzy to pay for the pensions of their baby-boomer parents, they would prefer to take it easy and grow some spuds. The Achilles heel of the protirers, however, is that their new lifestyle is sustained not by the spuds but the money they made on selling their house to move to the country – or from the fat inheritance bequeathed by Daddy. Without a private income, the protirer should be warned that there is a good chance that he will end up back in the office with his tail between his legs – and at a lower rung on the management ladder.

Public Value

Nowadays, every time the staff of the British Broadcasting Corporation wheel out a bid for a pay rise, they sugar their demand with the claim that they are busy providing 'public value'. The origins of this sticky, gelatinous substance called 'public value' tells us a great deal about the dilemmas facing our public institutions.

Although the last several decades have seen market mechanisms slowly intrude into almost every aspect of the public sector, there is still no easy way of measuring the performance of public sector workers according to market criteria. Back in 1995, a Harvard professor and management guru called Mark Moore tried to solve the problem in a book entitled *Creating Public Value: Strategic Management in Government*, which revolutionized thinking about how public managers should go about their business and assess the efficiency of their work. Given that the public sector cannot have its work measured by the profits it makes or the amount its customers are prepared to pay, the idea of public value was designed to fill the gap with an organizing principle for what public sector professionals and organizations do. Soon it was being pilfered by public bodies of all kinds as a way of bolstering their morale and justifying their budgets.

So it was that in 2004, when the BBC's executives were

sweating over how to argue for renewal of its charter and the protection of the licence fee, they turned up with a document headed 'Building Public Value'. 'Public value is a measure of the BBC's contribution to the quality of life in the UK,' pronounced the corporation's position paper. Indeed it may be, but it is just as likely that the BBC has been sold an intellectual pup. Whatever it says, public value cannot be measured quantitatively without lapsing into absurdity and is, therefore, of much more limited use than the theory of value that is used to analyse the market economy.

According to the laws of conventional economics, to which the public value idea is keen to adhere, public bodies are only allowed to intervene to produce public value in order to repair instances of market failure. As the textbook definition of market failure is the inability to absorb the unintended side-effects of any activity (called 'externalities') into the price mechanism, the BBC's boffins have been looking high and low for anything that might fit the bill. Its mixed bag of side-effects include the idea that the BBC might help reinvigorate local communities, and the notion that citizens who switch on to watch pure entertainment might press the wrong button and watch something intelligent instead.

The 'public value' dug up by the BBC thus far is negligible. It should concentrate on the intrinsic value of its programming rather than any amorphous wider benefits. The best way to justify its output would be to concentrate on a more contemporary kind of market failure – to contrast its ability to take long-term programming risks with the jittery and craven short-termism that plagues the world of shareholder-value driven broadcasting. Otherwise we might return the favour by paying our licence fees in treacly dollops of public value.

Regretful Loners

'Why am I being selfish if there's only me?' demanded singleton Will Freeman in Nick Hornby's determinedly sentimental novel *About a Boy*. Well, now we know. There was a brief moment, around the end of the last millennium, when singletons seemed to be out and proud, when the 'solo pound' promised to rejuvenate our inner cities, and when the single masses seemed to be about to join battle to overturn every oppressive social institution from single supplements to Valentine's day.

If it ever really existed, that moment is now over. A report published late in 2006 dubbed British people living on their own – and especially men between the ages of twenty-five and forty-four – as 'regretful loners' who consume more energy and generate more waste than couples. It was not the first piece of news to pour cold water on the joys of single living. Singletons are now regularly warned that their lives are lonely, miserable and short. Single men, according to a clutch of surveys, don't go to the doctor enough, are more likely to get depressed and – worst of all – have no one with whom to discuss their emotional problems. They are also, according to recent scientific research, more likely to have heart attacks, angina and suffer a sudden death. If heart disease doesn't get them, the social stigma surely will. In Japan, the backlash is such that young singletons are now tarred with the media brush of 'parasite singles'.

The burgeoning number of singletons, however, is too complex a problem to be solved by name-calling. Increased life expectancy means growing numbers of people are widowed and living alone and a rising divorce rate has increased the numbers of men and women content to live on their own – what market-eers call the 'seasoned singles'. The number of single-person households is also increasing because of the tendency for those in their twenties and thirties to postpone or shy away from coupledom. Where once settling down was the norm and single-ness a transitional state between relationships, as one report from the Economic and Social Research Council has it, nowadays it is marriage and couplehood that is the interlude: a pleasurable but easily disposable experience, to be moved on from as soon its participants revert to their default state of living alone.

To label this lot as 'regretful loners' is a little patronizing, but closer to the truth than fluff about the wonders of single living. Most young singles do aspire to a lasting relationship under one roof, but are balancing that aspiration against other considera-tions. The vogue for living alone among young professionals seems to be evidence of a more general development – that single-tons have begun to think of privacy as freedom from demands made by other people.

The question is what to do about it all. Policy wonks argue that 'regretful loners' should be encouraged to move into 'collective housing schemes' – glorified dormitories, in other words – but that seems unlikely to appeal. As most singletons live in glorified urban rabbit-hutches anyway, with less space and less need for a car than suburb-dwelling families, they are hardly the grotesque offenders against the environment that the report suggests. No, the worst thing about singletons is that they harbour an irrational fear of the harmful effects that might result from prolonged exposure to other people. Hardly selfish, but possibly just a little sad.

Resilience

In the aftermath of any terror attack in a Western country now, one word is repeated like a mantra. Immediately after the terror attacks on London's transport system on 7 July 2005, for example, the then British Prime Minister Tony Blair paid tribute to 'the stoicism and resilience of the people of London'. A couple of hours later, interviewed on Channel 4 News, Brian Paddick, Deputy Assistant Commissioner of the Metropolitan Police, assured viewers that the emergency services 'had sufficient resilience to cope'.

All this is a lovely compliment, but these terror attacks were not the first time our resilience was tested. Even before then, it had become one of the hottest buzzwords among military and business analysts. Since 11 September 2001, the Ministry of Defence has been busy commissioning all manner of research into the resilience of our big cities in the event of a terrorist attack. Boffins at the Strategy Unit of Number 10 have written countless turgid reports on what 'resilience' means. Cranfield University has even set up a whole research centre dedicated to understanding it.

The impetus behind all this interest in resilience is the conviction that organizations of all kinds need to do more to anticipate high-impact, low-probability disasters – whether natural, accidental or deliberate. Resilience gurus start with the assumption that because modern societies are much more networked and interdependent than those that went before, they are especially vulnerable to system breakdown. The one exception is usually said to be the new technologies, such as mobile phones and the internet; as networks such as these lack an organizational centre, runs the argument, they are much harder to disrupt. As a consequence, many of the suggestions made for fortifying our resilience are about remaking everything in their image: making everything more flexible and more diffuse. In his recent book *The Resilient Enterprise*, for example, the MIT professor Yossi Sheffi argues that companies can become more resilient by decentralizing operations and building flexibility into everything they do, so that a single shock to the corporate system does not have to precipitate its collapse. Rejig your company's operations in this way, Sheffi advises, and you can even steal a competitive march on your rivals. In the right hands, the threat of disaster can be an opportunity for innovation.

This is all very well, but while the targeting of the London bomb attacks near mainline stations was a bold attempt on the part of the bombers to take out key transport routes and cause maximum disruption to the urban metabolism, Londoners nevertheless remained calm and went about their business. Likewise, terrorism has turned out to be but a flea on the elephant of our economy, which was hardy enough to bounce back within a matter of hours. The irony of all the talk about the resilience of flexible networks, however, is that the technology fell flat on its face. According to a report into the bombings, rescuers could *not* use their radios underground, nor communicate with each other via their different radio systems. Those who relied on mobile phones found the system overwhelmed by the huge volume of calls shooting through it as Londoners tried to reach family members. The network failed to take the strain.

The ability of a huge metropolitan organism like London to withstand atrocity, the 2005 London bombs taught us, knows few bounds. If only the gadgetry were as reliable. The real lessons to be learned from all this are that we should be wary of learning too many knee-jerk lessons from catastrophes; that Londoners have always been resilient, and hardly need anyone to flatter their stoicism; that a highly integrated metropolitan population like London can quickly close ranks and withstand more than it thinks; and that we are more resilient when we get through things together, rather than when we split everything up.

Slacktivism

Want to feel good with the minimum of effort? Why not sit at home and sign petitions on the internet? E-petitions are only the most shameless manifestation of slacktvism, the twenty-first-century ghost of the mass movement politics which shook the twentieth century. In a single afternoon, the militant slacktivist can support myriad boycotts of unethical companies, forward endless appeals on behalf of dying children, and demand (with copious exclamation marks) an end to Western interference in the Middle East. That most of these 'e-petitions' – being unverifiable – have no influence whatsoever on the activities of governments or multinationals and end up in the bin need not trouble the slacktivist one iota. He has done his bit, and can go back to bed with a clear conscience.

Slacktivism, the phrase itself a rather lazy haemorrhaging of the two words 'slacker' and 'activism', is the counter-intuitive idea that armchair warriors can somehow change the world and topple its complacent political classes without even rising from their chairs. In the UK, for example, an underground army of slacktivists is driving the latest literary trend – a slew of reasonably priced books offering tips on how to make a difference. *Change the World for a Fiver* (2004), for example, outlines fifty modern commandments on how to bring about global justice – such as smiling, planting a tree and learning some good jokes. The Armchair Environmentalist, meanwhile, offers a 'can-do' approach to saving the planet, one which includes buying low-energy light bulbs and reusing envelopes.

In France, the slacktivist ethic takes the form of a radical laziness at work. The *Das Kapital* of the movement is economist Corinne Maier's 2004 bestseller *Bonjour Paresse* ('Hello Laziness'), a book whose unique recipe for workplace resistance is to do the least possible work and, in the words of Maier, 'screw the system from within without anyone noticing'. In the United States, slacktivists prefers to propagandize from the comfort of their couch or computer, usually donning their pyjamas for the job. 'Not One Damn Dime Day', for example, takes place once a year, and is, according to its sponsors, an opportunity to speak out against the war by boycotting all forms of consumer spending for twenty-four hours. What the slacktivist lacks in productivity, he or she makes up for in self-righteousness. Another slactivist protest, beloved by some American heterosexual liberals, is to protest against prohibitions on gay marriage by refusing to tie the knot.

The problem with slacktivism, the ultimate in easy-to-do, feel-good politics, is that its methods are indistinguishable from simply doing nothing. This is the politics of having a sulk. Far from being radical, its idea that the political urge can be satisfied by simply pressing a button or filling out a form is the ultimate in mind-numbing consumerism. Its efforts are unlikely to disturb the sleep of anyone, not even the slactivist himself.

Smart Mobs/Flash Mobs

When the young Prince William was studying for his art history degree at the University of St Andrews back in 2001, he suddenly began to face regular onslaughts from a curiously well-organized army of star-struck young female students. What were their weapons? Eventually, an intrigued Scottish reporter followed them around and discovered their modus operandi. 'A sophisticated text-messaging network has sprung up,' one campus insider confided. 'If William is spotted anywhere in the town then messages are sent out. It starts off quite small. The first messages are then forwarded to more girls and so on. It just has a snowball effect. Informing 100 girls of his movements takes seconds.'

Such 'swarming' behaviour among lustful students – using the exchange of mobile data as a means to faster coordination – is a frivolous example of how the new communication technologies can change the pace of social interaction. The speed at which this kind of mobile coordination takes place has suggested to some that it might spark social and political change. In his book *Smart Mobs: The Next Social Revolution* (2002), for example, futurologist Howard Rheingold described an emerging phenomenon in which people 'cooperate in ways never before possible because they carry devices that possess both communication and computing capabilities'. Rheingold used the example of the use by protesters of mobile phones during the riots at the 1999 WTO meeting in Seattle to coordinate their activities. Another striking example is often said to be the way in which coordination through text-messaging was instrumental in the public demonstrations which forced Philippines President Joseph Estrada from office in January 2001. During the four days of uprising which ended with Estrada's fall, SMS messages were used to keep protesters abreast of events as they unfolded, and to mobilize citizens to march, bring food and maintain a vigil. Although the traditional media were covering events freely and aggressively, they failed to keep pace with the speed at which information sent by text-message darted through large groups and motivated them to action.

In their haste to declare a new era, however, techno-enthusiasts like Howard Rheingold often fetishize the technology and exaggerate their case. There remains, however, a largely latent potential that coordination through mobile might give form to the expression of already existing social and political interests. In countries where information is strictly controlled, for example, the ubiquity of mobiles could pose a direct threat to the existing order. During a strict media and political blackout about the existence of SARS in China in 2003, for example, many Chinese people heard of the virus first through their mobile phone. As a direct result of the epidemic of texting, the media and subsequently the Chinese government were forced to admit the existence of the virus.

For the most part, however, the technology for mobile coordination has not spurred anything politically useful at all. Perhaps that it is why it has spawned a wayward younger brother in the notion of the 'Flash Mob'. The first flash mob was orchestrated back in June 2003 by a louche American journalist called Bill

Wasik, who sent an email to sixty friends and acquaintances as a result of which one hundred people converged on the rug department of Macy's department store, gathered around one very expensive rug and pretended to be shopping on behalf of the same 'free love' hippie commune. Since then, Wasik's experiment has been repeated around the world many times, its popularity only slightly dented by his confession in 2006 that it had all been an attempt to poke fun at journalists who spent their time greedily hunting new urban trends. The flash mob, like the smart mob before it, turned out to be something of a media-exaggerated flash in the pan.

Social Jet Lag

Feeling sluggish at the office, and skulking around in a disorientated daze? According to research unveiled by the best German sleep physicians, you might well be suffering from an ailment called social jet lag.

Social jet lag is said to arise when our body clock falls out of sync with the demands of our environment, thus putting us at risk of chronic fatigue and an increased susceptibility to disease. According to the hefty social survey produced by researchers in Munich, there is a mismatch of at least two hours between most of our biological clocks and the demands of our jobs. Up to half the population is in a permanent state of jet lag, they say, a condition exacerbated by poor office lighting and the tendency of office workers to spend their lunchtimes eating flaccid sandwiches while sitting at their desks. The solution, say the researchers, is to match our natural sleep rhythms more harmoniously to our daily routine: the average person, apparently, prefers to sleep between half past midnight and 8.30 in the morning.

Whatever else it claims to be, social jet lag sounds like a great excuse for arriving at work late. It is, however, just the quirkiest prong of an intriguing new train of scientific thinking that investigates ways in which the human body no longer fits into its surroundings. In their recent book *Mismatch: Why Our World No Longer Fits Our Bodies* (2006), for example, two scientists named Peter Gluckman and Mark Hanson argue that we have created an artificial world that is increasingly out of tune with the bodies that are our genetic inheritance. The idea that many of us would spend vast quantities of time shaking our limbs in gymnasiums would, a century ago, have provoked the ridicule of manual workers whose physically demanding jobs meant they were hardly in need of a workout. In the same way, as Gluckman and Hanson point out, there is a mismatch between the demands of the female biological clock – which prefers to get pregnant at a young age – and the cultural preference of many women to start families later in life.

The 'mismatch paradigm', they claim, happens anywhere where biology and environment begin to push in different directions. Humans are ingenious at adapting to a huge variety of different environments, note the authors, but a constant need to adapt is a source of stress which may be harmful. 'The greater the degree of match between an organism's constitution and its environment, the more likely the organism is to thrive,' say the authors. 'The greater the degree of mismatch, the more the organism has to adapt or cope.'

The relationship between our genes and our environment is a complex business, but the good news is that we are quite capable of making a difference to both. Given the strides we have already made in building a human environment, there is nothing to stop us from changing it around a bit more to give our bodies a better fit.

We could modify our genes, too, but the gene therapies that will help us to do so won't be up and running for a while. In the meantime, we need cleverer fixes. We could install artificial sunlight in buses, trains and offices, for example, or glass roofs to give us more natural sunlight. We could invent more efficient ways of topping up the nutrients our bodies need, or more interesting and useful ways of exercising those bodies than wasting valuable time in the gym.

Social Networking

The real money to be made out of the worldwide web, it turns out, was never in sex or shopping but in the simple act of bringing people together. The internet's second coming, it is now universally agreed, is taking its inspiration from the rise of so-called 'social networking sites' such as MySpace and YouTube, in which people chat with and open up their lives to perfect strangers.

MySpace now boasts over 70 million members. If it were a television programme, it would be the most popular and valuable in American history – which is why Rupert Murdoch shelled out nearly $600 million to buy it. The boom in social networking sites, however, is not confined to America. The British, according to a survey published in March 2006 by Google, now spend more time on the internet than watching television. Rather than stare mutely at a box in the corner, they would prefer to check each other out online.

All this is said to be a testament to the dazzling power of new social networks. Network theory is a bristling addition to the social sciences, drawn from mathematics and computing and beginning to assume almost cosmological significance. Sociologists at the Pew Research Center in America, for example, have recently drawn attention to a phenomenon called 'networked individualism', a new kind of community in which people find their social ties less within local groups than in geographically scattered networks. Americans might go bowling alone, to paraphrase Robert Putnam's famous argument about the atomized nature of modern American life, but when they go home they surf together.

If the twentieth century was shaped by people power, the twenty-first is already being moulded around the power of the network. The radical Italian intellectual Antonio Negri argues that networks in the form of nomadic new social movements operating on a global scale will shortly become the gravediggers of twenty-first-century capitalism. Even terrorists are not immune from changes in intellectual fashion. In a recent essay, the German thinker Hans Magnus Enzensberger characterized al-Qaeda as 'a flexible network: a highly original innovation that is entirely of its time'. The National Security Agency, the *New York Times* has reported, is also using network theory to try to understand the modus operandi of Islamist terrorists. As networks are diffuse and lack a centre, however, they are often said to be impressively resilient and almost impossible to destroy.

But are networks really so resilient? Some of what we call networks are as fragile as leaves in an autumn wind. MySpace could lose its cachet and its patrons overnight, just as its predecessor, Friendster, lost out to MySpace several years ago. As a political organizing tool, too, networks are deeply unreliable. When Howard Dean, that briefly hyped candidate for the US Democratic presidential nomination back in 2004, tried to build a mass movement around a website, it quickly lost momentum and his campaign fell flat on its face.

Turning up its nose at both geography and the nation-state, social networks are the perfect accompaniment to that opaque soup of ideas known as globalization. They are poor solace for more sustained kinds of democracy. Maybe we would be better off if we stopped stealing metaphors from science and computing to explain social phenomena. Nodes on the network we may be, but we remain strangers all the same.

Social Physics

How can the laws of physics help to explain how society works? Think about how a crowd fills up a stadium at a football match. If we were to measure the swelling of a crowd of football fans, it wouldn't be much use adding up the intentions of each fan. The motion of the crowd is more like the movement of interdependent particles of gas, and can be mapped in a similar way. By keeping everything else constant and varying external pressures – a ticket barrier at the football stadium, say – 'social physics' is capable of predicting quite complex patterns of collective movement.

The idea that the laws of physics can explain society is as intriguing as it is novel. It also comes in handy. The modern discipline of economics, after all, treats people as discrete and atomized individuals who are only out for what they can get. Within the 'softer' social sciences like sociology, on the other hand, individuals are often stuck together in a kind of formless glue, mutually suffocated by the weight of culture and tradition. Physics, on the other hand, is more interested in the collision between objects than in the objects themselves. Since society is more than the sum of its parts, many have begun to think that physics can fill a gap and help explain the consequences of human interaction.

One of the staunchest and most articulate advocates for a 'social physics' is the British science writer Philip Ball. In his book *Critical Mass: How One Thing Leads to Another* (2004), Ball presents us with aerial views of the way a throng of visitors fills up a crowded art gallery, or the way that cars move along a crowded motorway. Because the direction which each art lover takes is determined by a subtle negotiation with each of his fellows, and because each driver on the motorway modifies his speed in response to what the driver ahead does, he concludes that there are some things which cannot be reduced to the sum of individual actions and which can only be understood within groups. Collective social processes, he argues, can be seen to have their own physical laws of shape and form. A long line of cars on a motorway, for example, can be seen as a relatively stable physical body. But just as steam abruptly condenses to water, or snow-flakes suddenly appear when water vapour freezes into ice, a random movement by one car can convert the whole entity into a congested state.

Ball wants to press his 'social physics' in the service of improving the human condition. The idea that the methods of physics and the other natural sciences might help us understand human affairs, he points out, is a natural outgrowth of the heady ambitions of Enlightenment thought. Besides, the more we understand about the instinctive ways in which humans move around their shared environment, the better equipped we are to tilt things in a favourable direction: to reduce traffic congestion, for example, or overcrowding at football matches.

The problem with Ball's attempt at a social physics is that it is not very ambitious at all. Whereas the frigid templates of modern economics tend towards reassuring equilibria, Ball's idea of 'phase transitions' is biased in the direction of social anarchy and the idea that small events can have disproportionate consequences. But all this goes with the peculiar terrain which Ball and his peers have made their own, the analysis of crowding and the statistical tyranny of small decisions. Their preoccupations suggest that society is a terrifying, amorphous mass, subject to random and violent fluctuations, and that change can only be achieved at the margins, with a wave here and a nod there to ease things along. The allegory of 'social physics' is a suggestive one but – faced with anything more profound than a football match or a traffic jam – it almost immediately runs out of steam.

Soft Power

Speak softly, and carry a big carrot. For decades, even Europe's friends chuckled at this parody of its timid approach to foreign policy adventures. In its dealings with Iran over its nuclear ambitions, however, Europe has been promoting the embrace of 'soft power' as an exciting new tool for diplomacy.

Soft power is to the American military machine what the idea of the new man is to traditional masculinity. It is, according to the new European catechism, a more civilized way of doing things – one based on rational argument, proper procedure and bureaucratic haggling. In an only partly light-hearted article for the journal *Foreign Policy* in 2004, one analyst identified Europe as the world's first 'soft' or 'metrosexual' superpower. 'Metrosexuals', he argued, 'always know how to dress for the occasion (or mission). Spreading peace across Eurasia serves US interests, but it's best done by donning Armani pinstripes rather than US army fatigues.'

The idea of 'soft power', however, is not a European but an American invention, and it is not just about wearing Armani suits but about winning hearts and minds through cultural influence. For over a decade, Joseph Nye, a Professor of International Relations at Harvard and one of America's leading foreign policy thinkers, has been arguing that America should devote more time to exporting its culture – its language, values and brands – and promoting the country as a beacon of prosperity and openness. Watching the progress of the war on terror, Nye has argued that America's military belligerence after 9/11 was beginning to suffocate the soft power that traditionally made it attractive to foreigners.

Yet a funny thing has happened to Nye's idea on its way into the contemporary political vocabulary. In the past few years, Europe has quietly been rebranding itself to make political capital out of global anti-Americanism. Where America is deemed to have reverted to an evangelical Protestantism underwritten by George Bush, Europe offers itself as a secular oasis. Where America's armies strut around the world in search of a Pax Americana, Europe has borrowed Nye's idea to present itself as a connoisseur in the art of soft power. For the past few years, bogged down in an intractable war in Iraq, America has been happy to let Europe have its way over Iran. It has politely exited the ring, occasionally cheering on the efforts of Britain, France and Germany to find a diplomatic solution.

The problem is that there is little in the way of common culture and identity to which Europe can encourage others to aspire. Europe's 'softness', for what it is worth, seems to derive from its skills as a negotiator. A cynic might conclude that, rather than skilfully massaging the situation with its soft power, Europe is merely a softie, whose whispered overtures to the Iranians depend on having America's bad cop in the background. Stick with us, European leaders have seemed to be saying to the Iranians for the past two years – you wouldn't want to be left alone with my hot-headed friend across the water. But, very soon, it looks like they might.

Status Anxiety

Going anywhere special on holiday this year? Maybe you've chanced upon a volcanic island in the Galapagos archipelago, a beautiful ravine in Bhutan or some undiscovered shrine in Nepal? Just be sure everyone else hasn't beaten you to it. Holidaying off the beaten track has never been so tricky. The market for package holidays to familiar European destinations is still buoyant, but increasing numbers of people are looking further afield.

Once it was professional adventurers, such as Magellan or Columbus, who went in search of undiscovered territories to make them just like home. Now holidaymakers travel the world in search of something different, and to get away from everyone else. Therein lies the problem. When holidaymakers make it their mission to discover some unspoilt natural beauty, they throw themselves like lemmings into the 'positional economy'.

The positional economy was the concept dreamed up by a brilliant economist called Fred Hirsch, who presented it in his 1976 book *Social Limits to Growth*. Environmentalists talk about impending natural scarcities, but Hirsch drew attention to a more intriguing phenomenon – social scarcity, or things whose supply is limited not by nature but by social crowding. In modern societies, argued Hirsch, many of the goods that we seek are by their very nature positional – having the best haircut in the class, for example, or the nicest view of the lake from our country house, for example – because, since we are all pushing through the same narrow turnstile, they are impossible for everyone to achieve. The result is to pit everyone against everyone else, in a fruitless jockeying for position. When a product becomes positional, argued

Hirsch, those who want it end up spending more and more money in a kind of pointless social competition – pointless because one person's success in getting their hands on it diminishes the chances of everyone else. As our basic needs for food, clothing and shelter are met by the proliferation of material goods, Hirsch argued, more of the things we want have a collective or public character and become susceptible to this kind of social crowding. As pawns in the positional economy, we spend more and more time on a treadmill, running frantically to stay still, out of puff and out of pocket.

But the question of what qualifies as a positional good has never been properly answered. The most obvious example would be driving a car where roads are few and far between: if everyone drives at the same time, they all work against each other and traffic barely moves. Another example is fame: if everyone gets famous, fame ceases to be worth having, a lesson lost on the *Big Brother* brigade.

How widespread Hirsch's positional goods are is a moot point. In his recent book *Status Anxiety* (2004), Alain de Botton sought to apply it to almost everything, but one area where it seems to work very well is in the market for country cottages or exotic holidays. Since the supply of unspoilt beauty is limited, my lakeside holiday cottage with a pristine view of nothing but water, mountains and sky is diminished when everyone else arrives to build their own cottages. Prices rise, and those with deep pockets seek to outdo each other by searching for the most exotic land-scape, a relentless battle for position that is bound to leave almost everyone disappointed.

Much the same applies to those ever-more exotic holiday destinations, whose value diminishes as soon as I spy Jim from

Big Ideas STATUS ANXIETY

Accounts through my complimentary binoculars. Far better if everyone did their bit to alleviate social scarcity and packed their bags for Torremolinos.

The Support Economy

When intellectuals gripe about the brutality of twentieth-century ideologies, they should save a mention for the dangerous gospel of DIY – its sordid legacy of wilting MDF and iron-willed determination to undermine the interiors of our housing stock in a couple of decades. Like those hippies you find at Camden Market who think hangers twisted into interesting shapes make for an exciting product line, many of us were hypnotized into thinking that DIY was not only good for our wallets but good for our souls too. Add the fact that many of us had shelled out all our money getting a mortgage on a shoebox and couldn't stretch to have someone decorate it, and it was easy to see the attraction.

No more. In the course of 2006, profits in the DIY sector of the British economy were down by a whopping £6 million. The first sign of trouble was when Britain's biggest DIY chain B&Q decided to drop its trademark 'You can do it if you B&Q it' tagline as a botched job. Putting a brave face on figures that showed that his chain's first-quarter profits had nosedived by 70 per cent in 2006, B&Q's chief executive, Ian Cheshire, said the future 'was all about home improvement, not DIY'. The revamped B&Q now offers to install your furniture and decorate your house. It has even been to Poland to source the best tradesmen.

For two American business gurus, none of this will come as a surprise. Ever since their 2003 book *The Support Economy*, the husband-and-wife double-act, James Maxmin and Shoshana Zuboff, have argued that modern consumers are overburdened with choice and crying out for someone to help them navigate the complexities of modern life and do things for them. A chasm has opened up, the pair maintain, between the impersonal, cookie-cutter logic of the modern corporation and the increasingly individual habits of the modern consumer. Liberated into plenty by mass consumption, today's consumers want more than cheap goods and derisory customer service. Instead, they are clamouring for organizations that can be trusted to act on their behalf. As they languish on telephone helplines waiting for corporations to catch up, they are losing patience.

In the coming DFY (Do For You) economy, say Maxmin and Zuboff, many of us will prefer to outsource the running of our lives and will be happy to pay for the privilege. So significant is this shift, they claim, that we are witnessing a transition to a new stage of capitalism – from a service economy towards a support economy. In the emerging support economy, companies club together in giant federations to take responsibility for every aspect of consumption experience. Products will soon be neither here nor there; the process becomes the product.

This idea has attracted the attention of our leaders: on one of their recent visits to London, Maxmin and Zuboff stopped off to give the British government's Strategy Unit tips on how to reform public services. It is also throwing up opportunities for canny utility companies and well-known brands, who are queueing up to 'do for you'. Short of a babysitter or a dog-walker? Handyman businesses will soon spring up all over the place, offering to do everything from fix your toilet seat to disentangle your flatpacked IKEA shelves. They could start by making good the hash you made of the bathroom tiles.

Synthetic Worlds

In a scarcely reported move early in 2006, the makers of the online medieval role-playing game World of Warcraft reluctantly allowed teams of openly gay players, introducing the battle for sexual equality into the virtual world. Players had begun to organize gay pride marches within the game, apparently, which must have raised eyebrows among the more conservative wizards and elves.

Computer and video games are now big business. Their growing importance has been recognized by the British Academy of Film and Television Arts, which has announced that they are henceforth to be regarded as an art form alongside film and TV. The real action, however, lies in vast online role-playing games such as World of Warcraft, The Sims Online and Second Life, which are spreading like wildfire; World of Warcraft alone boasts 5.5 million players around the globe. The fantasy worlds they conjure up are breathtakingly elaborate, vast enough to include entire economies and class systems, and intelligent enough – riddled with their own rituals, symbols and language – to capture the attention of young adults as well as teenagers. They are also enormously addictive. In September 2007, a young Chinese man was reported to have collapsed and died after a three-day online game-playing session in an internet cybercafé. So worried are the Chinese authorities about the problem that they are trying to force online gaming sites to dock the points of gamers who stay online too long.

Edward Castronova, an online gamester turned Associate Professor at Indiana University, dislikes the tired metaphor of virtuality and prefers to calls these alternative universes 'synthetic worlds'. In his book of the same title, he argues that they have grown so powerful and their architecture so intricate that they are now in direct competition with our daily lives. As many of us begin to spend as much time in these make-believe worlds as the real one, Castronova sees the relationship between real and synthetic worlds becoming increasingly blurred, leading to clashes between the two. Not only does the outside world influence the synthetic worlds – as in the campaign for gay teams in Warcraft – but, conversely, events inside these games are increasingly rippling into the world outside. The fact that property is virtual, for example, has not been a bar to court cases being fought over its theft: in 2006 an American lawyer and virtual real-estate speculator on Second Life filed a lawsuit against Linden Lab for confiscating some of his virtual property.

Neither does the absence of virtual taxation mean that there is no taxation to be paid in the real world. People who take cash out of virtual economies are already required to report their incomes to the Internal Revenue Service in America. In the middle of October 2006, a US Congressional Committee confirmed that it was looking into the possibility of how better to levy taxes on the virtual income from economies like that of Second Life. Eventually a gravitational pull may draw all these virtual universes together, and common standards may emerge to enable their players to jump seamlessly from one to another. The result will be an online experience of truly global proportions and a synthetic world with vast financial clout.

Playing around in these alternative universes, Castronova notes, is less passive an experience than sitting on the couch watching television. If there are any political movements that want to appeal to gamers, he suggests, they would do well to make use of synthetic worlds to get their message across, in the same way that armies and some extreme right groups in the US have built computer games with which to push their world-view. The growing exodus or migration of young adults into these mythical worlds must reflect the tiresome, monotone worlds that the players inhabit in the real world. Their online existence, Castronova admits, 'is better than the alternative, that is, a daily life on Earth, which seems to show no progress towards anything'. Next time someone offers to cross your palm with a magic potion in return for some gold coins, take pity – it may not be a drug dealer but an online gamer in search of a life.

The Time Economy

It is a truth universally acknowledged that a cultural studies academic with any ambition is in want of an economy. Our university libraries are now weighed down with books on the economy of signs and signifiers, the economy of urban space, the economy of cultural prestige (see later), even the economy of our libidinal urges. Economies have currencies, whole populations and the suggestion that they are living and sentient; having one at our fingertips makes those of us in the arts or woollier social sciences sound scientific and rigorous. At its best, an economy can help to explain how a whole system of things works in perfect harmony. At its worst it can sound very silly indeed.

So it is with one recent contribution to the field, the economy of time. According to a survey published in 2006 by consumer analysts at the Henley Centre, the British value time more than they do money. Some 41 per cent of respondents to the survey mentioned time as their most valuable resource, while only 18 per cent believed that money was most important. The suggestion made by the surveyors is that many of us are permanently short of time, and that – as in a real economy – we might be prepared to trade off income in order to buy back more time. The rich can buy back time by hiring the poor to clean their houses or walk their dogs, whereas the poor can barely give it away. Everything depends on having enough money, but very few of us are hard-nosed enough to tell that to a passing surveyor.

More importantly, the implicit assumption that time should be treated like a scarce resource in a real economy is a little shaky. The notion that we are constantly under time-pressure, according to a different survey published by Mintel in 2004, is nothing but a myth. Working mothers aside, it is not true that most of us are working harder than ever before. Rising incomes give us the means to buy cheaper and more time-saving goods and appliances, and that in turn means that most of us have more time on our hands than ever before. Our cultural enthusiasm for ready-made meals, Mintel discovered, arose not because we had no time to cook properly but because we would rather trade that time in for more leisure time. Even when we are working, we seem to spend a large part of our working day chatting with colleagues and surfing the internet for cheap holidays.

But if the notion of time scarcity is an illusion, we do seem neurotic about how we spend our leisure time. In recent years, the Henley Centre has also identified a drift towards 'leisure canapés', in which people dip their toes in different leisure activities in order to squeeze as much as possible out of their free time. Such is the cornucopia of delights on offer that many of us end up unable to commit ourselves to anything. You don't have to be an apron-wearing, soup-stirring bore from the 'slow food' movement to wonder whether we could be less precious about the demands made on our time. Given that it is not as valuable as we think, perhaps we could afford to spend it more freely.

The Tipping Point

Everyone knows that things change, but how much do we know about that sudden moment when one thing changes into another? Interest in the point at which things 'tip' began in the early 1960s, when an American political scientist called Morton Grodzins noticed that white American families would stay put in their neighbourhoods so long as the number of incoming black families remained small. As more black families arrived, however, at a certain point the whites would suddenly flee the area en masse. It was Grodzins who christened that moment of dramatic change the 'tipping point'.

In the course of the 1980s and 1990s, the idea of the tipping point was borrowed to describe the point at which new technologies – the video or the mobile phone, for example – suddenly emerge from obscurity to overwhelm the popular imagination. At the beginning of the new century, however, it was dusted off and given a fresh lease of life by a gifted writer for the *New Yorker* called Malcolm Gladwell. Gladwell was impressed by Grodzins's work, but preferred to draw his metaphors from epidemiology. In his 2000 book *The Tipping Point*, Gladwell put forward the audacious idea that the best way to think about everything from changing fashions to the rise of teenage smoking was to imagine people as viruses and social phenomena as contagious epidemics.

Gladwell based his thesis on three related ideas. We need to be aware, he said, that huge changes can sometimes issue from small impacts or interventions; that sometimes these changes happen very quickly; and that sometimes only a tiny handful of people are instrumental in effecting the change. Take, he said, the crime rate in 1990s New York. During the 1980s New York was a crime-infested ghetto and many of its residents were afraid to go out at night. At a certain point, however, all that began to alter and the crime rate began to decline. Economists and sociologists trotted out explanations for why this might have happened, but they were at a loss to explain the suddenness of the change. The only way to understand it, says Gladwell, is to hone in on how the behaviour of some would-be criminals began to alter, and how that behaviour spread to other, similar situations. Somehow, he says, a large number of people in New York must have been infected by an 'anti-crime virus', a virus which just kept spreading.

Gladwell's *Tipping Point* was both intriguing and thought-provoking, but its pared-down approach to solving social problems quickly became a chancer's charter – press-ganged into service by just about anyone who wanted to turn around their public image, their crime problem or their marketing strategy on the cheap. The most enthusiastic audience for the tipping point, it turned out, were marketers whose traditional methods were beginning to look stale and out of date, and who wanted to start social epidemics of their own – 'word-of-mouth' or 'buzz' aimed at getting people to talk about their products. Gladwell helped by identifying the kinds of people who were most influential in powering his social epidemics: 'mavens' who make it their business to know products and who are keen to tell people what they know; 'connectors' whose job it is to pass information on; and 'salesmen', whose persuasive charms we often fail to resist. Gladwell the writer combines elements of all three, but his real talent as an ideas entrepreneur is as a salesman.

Transhumanism or The Singularity Thesis

Who wants to live for ever? Time was when only Michael Jackson and a few narcissistic billionaires imagined that they could cheat death with the help of some wacky and very expensive science. Recently, however, the idea of radically extending human life has found itself a more respectable audience. Chief among that audience is an informal movement of evangelists for radical life extension called transhumanism. What unites them is the belief that if we humans can just hang on for the next thirty or forty years, the science will have reached such a level of sophistication that we will be able to live for the next 1,000 years. The route to radical life extension will evolve through a series of 'bridges' to help us use our existing knowledge to slow down the ageing process, enabling today's middle-aged to stay healthy until advances in biotechnology and nanotechnology allow us to turn off ageing and disease.

The arrival of 'singularity', according to its inventor, the futurologist Ray Kurzweil, will arrive in 2045. Singularity, says Kurzweil, is a development 'representing a profound and disruptive transformation in human capability' and a 'radical upgrading of our bodies' physical and mental systems'. What are its elements? The first half of the twenty-first century, Kurzweil maintains, will be characterized by three overlapping revolutions: human genetics, robotics or artificial intelligence and nanotechnology. Biotechnology, rapid advances in genomics and gene therapies will enable us to turn off disease and ageing and thus we can live for much longer. Since we will soon be able to 'reverse engineer the brain' and simulate its functions, technology will increasingly merge with human intelligence to create something with greater capacity and speed. Nanotechnology, the science of small things, will enable us 'to redesign and rebuild – molecule by molecule – our bodies and brains and the world with which we interact, going far beyond the limitations of biology'. New technologies, Kurzweil recognizes, usually create new jobs for those displaced by it. Cloning, for example, is not as scary as it is made to sound, and might even offer solutions for world hunger, creating meat and other protein sources in a factory without animals by cloning animal muscle tissue.

Transhumanists share a welcome zeal for overcoming our human limitations, but we should take their claims with a pinch of salt. Technology, it is important to remember, conducts its way through society as a series of quantitative heaves rather than a qualitative leap. Kurzweil thinks that the exponentially increasing processing power of computers can help us understand the speed of social change. The changes he describes might look fast on paper, but they filter through to social life at a snail's pace. Many of them do not make it at all, because of a lack of investment or human enthusiasm.

Throughout his book Kurzweil capitalizes 'singularity'. He even has a name for someone who is a follower of the faith: 'I regard someone who understands the Singularity and who reflects on its implications for his or her own life as a "singularitarian".' He pays lip service to a kind of humanism – 'we will transcend biology, but not our humanity' – but sounds like a religious evangelist, or a West Coast new ager who has spent too long in front of a computer. For Kurzweil, all that remains is an ethical problem – how humanity adapts to the new post-singular world in which we have become outsmarted by machines. His metaphor of singularity plays well in the science-fiction community, among Hollywood scriptwriters in need of inspiration, and among military spooks whose job it is to think ahead of the curve. For us ordinary mortals, it is singularly unhelpful.

True Cost Economics

'Cut down your pollution and cash in', sounds a little too good to be true, but it is one of the ritzier attempts to solve our environmental problems. The idea, as floated by the British Environment Secretary David Miliband during a slow news week in the summer of 2006, was to force us all to carry a swipe card to record our personal carbon ration, with points deducted each time we buy petrol or flight tickets. The clever twist was that those who didn't use up their carbon allowance would be able to flog the spare points to those who want to blow a little more than their ration allows. Think of it as the opposite of air miles, with coupons chalked up by those who don't bother to get on the plane.

Miliband's policy wheeze was designed to make the British government look forward-thinking and audacious, but it was only the latest in a long line of attempts to bring economics into harmony with our environment. The goal of most of these schemes is to 'internalize the social costs' of our activities, so that the harm they cause is reflected in the amount everyone pays. Ideas like this are riding a wave of influence, not only among Western governments but among activists.

Take the True Cost Manifesto (truecosteconomics.org), an initiative from the radical Canadian anti-advertising magazine *Adbusters*. In its inaugural proclamation, its founders fulminate against the profession of economics. 'We, the undersigned,' they write, 'make this accusation: that you, the teachers of neoclassical economics and the students that you graduate, have perpetuated a gigantic fraud upon the world. You have known since its inception that your measure of economic progress, the gross domestic product, is fundamentally flawed and incomplete, and yet you have allowed it to become a global standard.' The only solution, claim the True Cost revolutionaries, is to 'reprogram the doomsday machine' by totting up the real costs of everything that we do.

This is spirited stuff, but the relationship between mainstream economics and the True Cost Manifesto is closer than its protagonists imagine. This kind of solution to problems of social cost owes its origins not to any radical guru but to a mainstream economist named Ronald Coase. Writing in 1960, long before the rise of environmental activism, Coase noticed that harmful effects caused by human action did not show up in the market, and that their presence meant a failure of the free market to organize our affairs. Coase's suggestion was to change the rules so that these harmful effects become commodities that are capable of being bought and sold too. If the flowers in my garden are taking their toll on your hay fever, for example, the solution would be for you to pay me not to grow them.

Coase's solution works best when harmful effects arise between only two parties – when the victim can simply bargain with the perpetrator for compensation. Whenever problems of social cost are more diffuse, such as pollution in which we are all both perpetrators and potential victims, the idea is that government can step in to establish artificial markets in 'permits to pollute'. But surely we have enough markets without adding a market in bad things? The result of all this would be to turn everything from the flowers that we grow to the fumes that we produce into a commodity with a price. Cash in the points on your carbon loyalty card by all means, but don't fool yourself that you're saving the world or shaking the economic system to its foundations. You're merely paying tribute to Ronald Coase's ingenuity.

Urban Gaming

Time was when playing computer games, a little like masturbation, was a solitary activity much enjoyed by adolescents and frowned on by everyone else. Not any more. The latest generation of computer games consoles from Sony and Nintendo, you might have noticed, are aimed at an adult audience which wants to play them communally rather than alone. It is not only computer games which are becoming more clubbable. In November 2006, a woman in a red wig and a Superman costume was spotted driving through the streets of Jacksonville, Florida. No refugee from the asylum, the woman was, together with nineteen other strangely dressed colleagues, busy deciphering some seventy-five clues, driving to different locations and continually checking her mobile phone – all in the pursuit of a very modern and yet strangely old-fashioned kind of urban game.

At least in America, urban gaming traditionally referred to the casinos and bingo parlours operated free of state regulation by Native Americans, a concession aimed at shoring up the flagging reservation system. Just recently, however, it has begun to refer to a wholly different kind of activity, one that combines the virtual world with the real-life geography of a modern city. A variety of new technologies – camera phones, wireless clouds of internet access, global positioning systems that allow you to track the path taken by yourself and your friends through the city – mean that computer games can now be tied firmly to location, bringing together communities of gamers or setting them against each other in games that unfold in the real world. The new kind of urban gaming began with players burying treasure and then posting the coordinates of the booty online to allow others to hunt for the prize. These kinds of modern treasure hunt are becoming very popular, played by thousands of people across the world and with prizes buried in ever more challenging locations.

One popular urban game in London is called Uncle Roy All Around You (www.uncleroyallaroundyou.co.uk), in which players use mobile devices to search for Uncle Roy, aided by maps and by messages from online players who guide them towards their destination. Developed by academic Steve Benford at the University of Nottingham, it challenges people to find 'Uncle Roy' by following instructions or clues given to them via mobile text-message, avoiding all the traps and red herrings which are placed in their way. Researchers in Singapore have even developed a version of the arcade game Pacman which grafts the game on to a real place by means of special goggles and headsets. Punters race around a dedicated play area collecting tiny energy pills and being chased by ghosts determined to kill them.

Each to their own. But the new urban gaming also tells us something interesting about how the internet has developed. Much of what has gone on in the worldwide web hitherto has been cocooned in the parallel world of cyberspace, but urban gaming promises to help tip the eccentric contents of the virtual world back into real life. It might even persuade internet nerds everywhere to exit their bedrooms and stretch their legs.

Urban Villages

Look out over central London on a clear day and there are villages as far as the eye can see. My own little hamlet, on the Old Kent Road in south-east London, hovers just on the edge of Bermondsey Spa Village, which is being tarted up after decades of neglect. Further down live the villagers of Peckham, who are rumoured to be a welcoming bunch.

The idea of urban villages comes with a distinguished heritage. In the early 1960s, the American sociologist Herbert Gans was investigating the Italian-American communities of Boston when he began to notice something significant. The way those communities used urban space, he argued, was a deliberate attempt to recreate the cosy everything-in-one-place feel of the southern Italian villages whence they came. What's more, he reckoned, American cities as a whole could be seen as a patchwork quilt of different villages in which non-urban immigrants tried to shape the city to look like the places they remembered from back home.

Gans's idea of the urban village was one in which communities were knitted together by shared ethnicity, but it has taken on a fresh lease of life at the beginning of the twenty-first century. Nowadays, the idea of the urban village is the brainchild of the 'new urbanism' architectural movement championed by the Prince of Wales, and it is one which has found official favour within governments almost everywhere in the West. For the architects and the politicians who have revived it, the idea of an urban village is about creating a neighbourhood in which everything is within walking distance, where people can work and shop in close proximity to where they live and play. Unlike the gasoline-guzzling maze of cul-de-sacs and population sprawl of suburbia, the urban village keeps cars at bay and boasts excellent transport connections. It is also a reaction against the ambitious high-rise developments that were popular in the 1960s, and which have now fallen into disrepute.

But the revival of the urban village is about much more than just policy. The growth of farmers' markets and other symbols of village life in our big cities suggests that many of us urban-dwellers are secretly hankering after a life in the country. Turning us all into urban villagers risks taking much of the excitement out of city life and returning us to a sleepy village idiocy that many of us left home to avoid. At its most basic, the idea of the urban village is just a gimmick, a foil for rebranding our inner cities as less forbidding and less anonymous places than we know them to be. Without any real work on urban infrastructure, many of today's urban villages – rather like the ethnic villages discovered by Gans – are just urban ghettos by any other name.

Virtual Anthropology

At one of the places I used to work, the receptionist had as her screensaver a live video image of wild animals lying around a cage in a zoo. On a different screen above her head, she was able to look at images from a bank of CCTV cameras of the whole building. Darting from one to the other, I suppose she might have discovered some similarities between the two.

Watching people on CCTV is now so common that it has ceased

to be controversial. Its success in helping convict criminals, and its sterling work in capturing just about every major crime or tragedy of the past decade, seems to have earned it our grudging respect. But CCTV also serves as a fuzzy, twentieth-century proto-type for a world in which many of us would prefer to spend our leisure time watching each other than doing anything else. Quietly, in the course of the last decade, many of us have quit watching the box in the corner of the room and disappeared off to the other room to fiddle around with gadgets – web cameras, mobile phones, or portable CCTV equipment – through which we can watch each other instead. It's just another way of frittering away our leisure time, though it can claim to be more social than television – we can use cameras to keep in touch with friends on the other side of the world, or to observe the baby sleeping upstairs, or to check on the weather in our favourite city. But it is also more private, because most of us are alone when we do it.

This is known as 'peer-to-peer' communication (see the entry on peer-to-peer surveillance), and it is widely acknowledged to be driving the future of the worldwide web more than anything else. Much of that 'communication' involves nothing more than simply observing each other. Our sex lives, for example, are increasingly migrating to a vast virtual menagerie in which people expose themselves on web cameras either for everyone to see or for the attention of someone special – or for a paying customer. Even when we do watch television, it increasingly resembles the same CCTV model. The potential insights this yields into human behaviour has not been lost on corporations. Trendspotters have recently identified a new science called 'virtual anthropology', where companies pay people to find out about their young customers by 'living' among them – perusing their online photos, reading their diaries, and peering at them through their web cams.

Being watched can have its psychological compensations, however. In his book *The Naked Crowd* (2004), the American academic Jeffrey Rosen argues that being noticed or exposed can help shore up one's identity in an age where people are less sure of who and what they are. 'Confused and anxious about status in a world where status is constantly shifting,' he concludes, 'we feel increasing pressure to expose details of our personal lives to strangers in order to win their trust, and we demand that they expose themselves in return in order to win our trust.' Watching each other on a screen, however, the danger is that we fail to apprehend the real world outside – that we become ghosts in the ether, staring mutely down copper pipes at each other, sometimes from only across the street, the watcher waiting for something to happen and the watched waiting to be noticed, both illuminating each other's solitude. It is no use blaming 'Big Brother' because, in the end, there is only us.

Virtual Politics

If you feel too confused about recent political events in Russia, Ukraine or Belarus even to offer a dinner-party opinion, don't fret. According to Andrew Wilson, an academic at London's School of Slavonic and East European Studies, we are perfectly right to be a little perplexed, because nothing is as it seems. In his book *Virtual Politics* (2005), Wilson argues that much of what passes for democratic participation in most of the countries of the former Soviet Union is entirely fake, a carefully choreographed performance designed to maintain the political status quo.

A decade ago, most political scientists liked to talk animatedly about 'post-Soviet transitions to democracy' as though this were a natural process in which they might lend a hand. Nowadays their mood is more circumspect. Following a brief flurry of popular protest in Russia and its neighbours after the implosion of the Soviet Union, Wilson argues, political elites entrenched their position and democratic impulses ossified into scorn for politics of all stripes. In a world in which a return to totalitarianism is considered unacceptable, virtual politics 'is the way that elites seek to manage, manipulate and contain democracy'.

How does it all work? The democratic process, according to Wilson, is choreographed by a cadre of 'political technologists' – many of whom learned their craft as apparatchiks in Soviet times. Whole parties and politicians are launched as TV projects, and then dropped as soon as they outlive their usefulness; electoral rolls are tinkered with; fake opinion polls and sociological surveys are drummed up to intimidate and demoralize opponents; 'shell parties' are regularly constructed out of thin air, and real parties cloned to confuse the electorate. Politicians are only avatars, says Wilson, like the easily clickable icons of cyberspace.

For the most part, Wilson's ire is directed at authoritarian governments in Moscow, Minsk and Kiev, but it might just as easily apply to the 'movements within civil society' that are sponsored not by Russia but by Europe and America. Western commentators, for example, became curiously dewy-eyed when Viktor Yushchenko won the Ukrainian election from the pro-Russian Viktor Yanukovych in the 'Orange Revolution' of 2004.

Now that the party of his former opponent has triumphed in recent parliamentary elections, however, many of them are lost for words. Likewise, the re-election of President Alexander Lukashenko in Belarus in March 2006 was widely and rightly condemned as fishy by Western governments, but it is often forgotten that he has a good deal more popular support than his opponents. In this new phoney war, democracy and civil society are the playthings not only of the FSB (the successor to the KGB), but of the CIA and MI6 too. Such is our inability to see through the political fog, according to Wilson, that the study of post-Soviet politics might soon revert to something similar to Kremlinology – the painstaking study of announcements and rituals that was used to divine what was really happening in the corridors of Soviet power. One way out of the shadows might be to agree a ceasefire on claims that one's own political clique is the authentic voice of 'civil society' – a scoundrel concept if ever there was one.

War Porn

In the summer of 2006, the US Army took the unusual step of demanding that its soldiers stop posting video clips on the web. They had good reason: the previous year, a minor scandal broke when it emerged that GIs were sending pictures of dead Iraqis to a website called www.nowthatsfuckedup.com in exchange for naked pictures of other men's girlfriends.

Little wonder, then, that the military men should be getting hot under the collar. Quietly, via the vast panoply of cables and copper wires that make up the worldwide web, and under the noses of the broadcast media, sites such as MySpace and YouTube are becoming the repository for gruesome images of war shot by American soldiers in Iraq and Afghanistan. The traffic in gory pictures works in both directions. Specialist sites such as Ogrish.com use sophisticated programs to monitor extremist jihadi websites to provide their customers with a vast super-market of images of death and dismemberment; at their most brutal, these clips show carefully choreographed execution videos such as that made of Ken Bigley. Most of us would rather not see such things, but many are taking a sneaky peek while no one else is around. On an average day, Ogrish claims to receive between 125,000 and 200,000 unique hits on its website; on a major news day, that can rise to 250,000.

What are we to make of this new battle over images? Fifteen years ago, the French social theorist Jean Baudrillard argued – with his tongue partly in his cheek – that the first Gulf war did not really exist but was a mirage conjured up by the broadcast media. More recently, in his 2004 essay 'War Porn', Baudrillard drew attention to the way in which the garishly explicit images of barbarity arriving from Iraq borrowed from the aesthetics and production values of modern porn. The posing of Iraqi inmates for those famous pictures in Abu Ghraib prison, he pointed out, shot on digital camera and originally intended only for private distribution, smacked of a kind of specialist, niche pornography. The photos, he argued, constituted 'the degradation, atrocious but banal, not only of the victims, but of the amateur scriptwrit-ers of this parody of violence'. There was no longer any need to 'embed' journalists in armies, declared Baudrillard, because the soldiers themselves have become so immersed in the media war.

'Due to their omnipresence, due to the prevailing rule of the world of making everything visible,' he intoned gravely, 'the images, our present-day images, have become substantially pornographic.'

War porn is designed not to titillate, but to humiliate its victims and horrify its audience. Like pornography, its producers heighten their sense of reality by videoing themselves in the act, while its audience does the same by ogling the videos. Grotesque new horror film series such as *Hostel* and *Saw* seem to be imitating war porn, which in turn has been inspired by movies. If the previous Gulf war seemed to exist only as a television spectacle, the new Iraq war can claim to be the first war fought by protagonists armed with digital cameras and access to the web. If the first existed only as a media-generated fantasy, this new one looks more like a pornographic nightmare.

Wild Card Theory or Black Swan Theory

London, 2010: in a city brought to its knees by cyberterrorism and the deliberate contamination of its water supply by Islamic militants, thousands of the newly jobless roam the streets stoking civil unrest while the armed forces stand by, powerless. Scotland and Wales secede from the UK and establish their own standing armies. England is alone and uniquely vulnerable. The Islamists, armed with sophisticated chemical and biological agents, move in for the kill.

The above is not the improbable plotline for a lavish Hollywood movie. It is the brainchild of boffins labouring on behalf of the Ministry of Defence. It is the very British equivalent of a new discipline called 'wild card' or 'black swan' theory, the latest innovation within military intelligence circles. These new theories put futurological boffins together with military spooks to brainstorm high-impact, low-probability disasters – those that are technically possible but extremely unlikely to happen. On the pages of his magazine the *Futurist*, for example, one of the world's leading future-thinkers, Edward Cornish, expounds the merits of the new approach. A wild card, he explains, is an unexpected event that has extremely important consequences for any particular individual or group. Wild cards 'have the power to completely upset many things and radically change many people's thinking and planning'.

In America, the big cheese in 'wild card' theory is John Petersen, head of a powerful American think tank called the Arlington Institute, which receives much of its funding from the US military. Petersen defines wild cards as 'punctuations in the systems. They disrupt the equilibrium.' Sometimes, he notes, 'they are the result of a series of events that, in and of themselves, have not produced any noticeable change – but, suddenly, boom! A wild card emerges out of the blue.' Petersen's *oeuvre* features plenty of boom, particularly since 11 September 2001. As well as dealing in run-of-the-mill disasters – the collapse of the United Nations, an attack by nuclear terrorists on the United States – Petersen is happy to discuss the possibilities of a second coming of the Messiah, the discovery of extraterrestrial life and even an outbreak of altruism all over the world.

Yet another variant on the same theme is 'black swan' theory, the invention of an enigmatic financial mathematician and Wall Street trader called Nassim Nicholas Taleb. Black swan theory, so-called because of the improbability of encountering a black swan in a group of white ones, argues that people systematically underestimate the inexplicable randomness of empirical data. In his new book *The Black Swan: The Impact of the Highly Improbable* (2007), Taleb argues for the role of high-impact random events in determining the course of history. Most people ignore 'black swans', Taleb believes, because they are more comfortable seeing the world as something structured, ordinary and comprehensible.

Both wild card theory and black swan theory would have languished in intellectual obscurity, of course, had it not been for the terrorist attacks on North America on 11 September 2001. For futurologists capable of imagining creative dystopias, the events of that day threw up a new employer in the intelligence agencies and an exciting new way of working. The chief occupational hazard of being a future-thinker, after all, has always been that one's predictions might prove to be wrong. But in a game of wild cards or black swans, it is hard to see how the future-gazer can lose. When the predicted disaster fails to show up, the futurologist can simply ask for a slap on the back for helping to prevent it.

Worst-Case Scenarios

Whatever happened to avian flu? Remember the dead duck, the discovery of whose flu-ridden corpse near Lyons in February 2006 sent the media into a frenzy? The following day came the news that a German cat had succumbed, and that the virus had leap-frogged from birds to domestic pets in Europe. A trail of almost biblical proportions seemed to have opened up to warn us of our fate, and there was little we could do but hunker down and wait for the inevitable. Millions of us could be dead in twelve months.

Nothing happened, of course. But see how easy it is to drift into speculating about the worst possible eventuality? Avian flu does not yet pose any direct threat to humans, but the worst-case scenario is that it might mutate and trigger a flu pandemic that would put millions of human lives at risk. An enthusiasm for ignoring the whole range of probabilities to fix on the worst possible outcome haunts the popular consciousness, and has been flummoxing social scientists for more than a decade. In Europe, it has been filed by portentous European sociologists like Ulrich Beck and Anthony Giddens under the heading of 'risk society'. In America, they just call it 'the dread factor'.

But according to the American sociologist Lee Clarke, author of *Worst Cases: Terror and Catastrophe in the Popular Imagination*, the dread factor is less irrational than we might think. Ushering us through a catalogue of near misses and outrageously unlikely accidents, Clarke contends that disasters are more normal than we believe, and that worst cases abound. He distinguishes worst-case thinking from the conventional approach of probabilistic thinking. The rationale of worst-case thinking, he says, explains why we're urged to wear seatbelts and not to smoke. To ignore worst cases would also be elitist, as it disregards lay opinions about how to calculate risk. Worst-case scenarios, he argues, can motivate us to action, protect us from hubris and teach us a little humility.

Clarke's argument is an intriguing one, but flawed. A decision-making rule that evaluates every course of action in terms of its worst possible outcome is already known to game theorists as the maximin principle, and it is common ground that it leads to perverse results. Imagine that I am simultaneously offered two jobs, one tedious and badly paid in London and another glamorous and lucrative in New York. The New York job means that I will have to fly there, and there is a small possibility that my plane might crash. Weighing up my options with the help of the maximin rule, I should prefer the London job, as the worst possible outcome of accepting the post in New York is that I wind up in an economy-class watery grave. The trouble with the maximin principle is that it means my decisions turn on a worst-case scenario irrespective of the likelihood of such a scenario ever coming to pass. Worst-case scenario dictates that when I next take a walk I will be run over by a double-decker bus. Worst-case scenario says that on a long-haul flight I will find myself sitting next to Richard Branson.

Worst-case scenarios need to be taken into account, as Clarke says, but they are not in themselves a reliable guide to action and should always be balanced against the likelihood that they will come to pass. Next time a bird flu panic comes along, before you stock up on antiviral medicine, shoot the cat and head for the hills, remember to take a deep breath and weigh up the odds.

Yeppies

Which of you can remember where you were when you first heard of the yuppie? I was eleven years old, sitting in the middle of the back seat of the car, when my mother swung around suddenly from the front seat. 'See those people?' she said, pointing at pedestrians walking briskly and bearing briefcases. 'They must be yuppies. Are you going to be a yuppie?'

Thankfully I wasn't. But one of the latest demographic acronyms to emerge from the marketing ether is scarcely more inviting. According to a report published by Oxford's Social Issues Research Centre, today's young people, aged between sixteen and twenty-four, are best characterized as Young Experimenting Perfection Seekers – or 'yeppies' for short. The yeppies are not single-mindedly materialistic enough to be yuppies. Instead, they believe that true personal fulfilment comes only after years of anguished experimentation. As a result, they feel entitled to behave like fickle consumers in everything that they do.

Just as they might browse the shops or flick through the pages of a lifestyle magazine, yeppies like to shop around when choosing jobs, careers, homes, identities and relationships. By trying on an assortment of different jobs and lifestyles, the yeppie wants to be flexible enough to change direction or to hit the reverse pedal when things do not work out. The yeppie might get trained up in a profession and then dither for a few years, writing a bad novel or becoming an eco-entrepreneur. He or she is happy to postpone all adult decisions until completely satisfied that all the options have been exhausted.

The drift towards life-shopping, according to the researchers, can explain the rise of the singleton. In 1971, the average age at first marriage was twenty-five for men and twenty-three for women. By 2003, this had increased to thirty-one for men and twenty-nine for women. The growth of the yeppie also helps to explain the 'boomerang' generation of young adults who, after a spell in the cold world of adulthood, head straight back to the family home. In 2004 around a quarter of women between the ages of twenty-five and twenty-nine and two fifths of men within that age group were still living with their parents.

By 2012, according to the Social Issues Research Centre, there will be an increasing acceptance of prolonged adolescence; it will be entirely normal for people – even those in their late twenties – to remain ensconced in the family home. Small wonder, then, that yeppies find it so difficult to settle down or to work at building a career. For all their vaunted nimbleness, the Achilles heel is their inability to grow up and knuckle down. Faced with any decision whose outcome is uncertain, they find themselves caught like a rabbit in the headlights. Unrealistically high expectations are also a burden. After all, why throw yourself into anything when something better might come along at any moment?

Your Ideas

Your Ideas

Your Ideas

Your Ideas

Your Ideas

Your Ideas

Your Ideas

Your Ideas

Your Ideas

Your Ideas